10 MINUTE GUIDE TO

WINDOWS NT™ WORKSTATION 4.0

by Sue Plumley

A Division of Macmillan Computer Publishing
201 West 103rd St., Indianapolis, Indiana 46290 USA

Dedicated to my dad, Ovis L. "John" Bender.

©1996 Que® Corporation

Library of Congress Catalog Card Number: 95-71747

International Standard Book Number: 0-7897-0870-1

98   8 7 6 5

Interpretation of the printing code: the rightmost double-digit number is the year of the book's first printing; the rightmost single-digit number is the number of the book's printing. For example, a printing code of 96-1 shows that this copy of the book was printed during the first printing of the book in 1996.

Printed in the United States of America

Publisher Roland Elgey

Vice President and Publisher Marie Butler-Knight

Publishing Manager Lynn E. Zingraf

Editorial Services Director Elizabeth Keaffaber

Managing Editor Michael Cunningham

Acquisitions Coordinators Stephanie Gould and Martha O'Sullivan

Product Development Specialist Lorna Gentry

Production Editors Katie Purdum and Tom Lamoureaux

Technical Specialist Nadeem Muhammed

Book Designer Kim Scott

Cover Designer Dan Armstrong

Production Team Marcia Brizendine, Jason Carr, Melissa Coffey, Joan Evan, Jessica Ford, Christine Pesetski, Donna Wright

Indexer Debra Myers

Special thanks to Discovery Computing, Inc. for ensuring the technical accuracy of this book.

WE'D LIKE TO HEAR FROM YOU!

As part of our continuing effort to produce books of the highest possible quality, Que would like to hear your comments. To stay competitive, we *really* want you, as a computer book reader and user, to let us know what you like or dislike most about this book or other Que products.

You can mail comments, ideas, or suggestions for improving future editions to the address below, or send us a fax at (317) 581-4663. For the online inclined, Macmillan Computer Publishing has a forum on CompuServe (type **GO QUEBOOKS** at any prompt) through which our staff and authors are available for questions and comments. The address of our Internet site is **http://www.mcp.com** (World Wide Web).

In addition to exploring our forum, please feel free to contact me personally to discuss your opinions of this book: on CompuServe, I'm at **75703,3251**, and on the Internet, I'm **lgentry@que.mcp.com**.

Thanks in advance—your comments will help us to continue publishing the best books available on computer topics in today's market.

Lorna Gentry
Product Development Specialist
Que Corporation
201 W. 103rd Street
Indianapolis, Indiana 46290
USA

CONTENTS

INTRODUCTION

Windows NT 4.0 provides a powerful yet easy-to-use operating system that enables you to use a variety of applications in addition to connecting to a variety of networks. The features and procedures of Windows NT are similar to those of Windows 95, but the power behind the application is supreme.

THE WHAT AND WHY OF WINDOWS NT WORKSTATION 4.0

Windows NT 4.0 is an exceptional operating system that enables you to perform tasks—such as opening programs, copying files, editing documents, and so on—that help you get your work done quickly and easily. In addition, Windows NT lets you connect to your company's network to access other computers, files, printers, and more.

Windows NT is a *graphical user interface* (GUI), which means that Windows provides a workspace that is graphical, and therefore, easy to use and easy to understand. As you become familiar with Windows NT, you'll find that it makes it easy to use applications effectively to manage your files.

 Graphical User Interface   A GUI (pronounced "gooey") makes interacting with your computer easy. You usually use a mouse to point at and select icons (small pictures that most often represent files or application programs), and you choose operations (commands from menus) to perform on those icons. A GUI is an alternative to a command-line interface such as DOS, where the user must enter text commands from the keyboard.

Why use Windows NT? Windows NT makes using your computer faster and easier in the following ways:

- You can work in and have several applications open on-screen at the same time if you like. You can also easily switch between open applications and share data between applications, both of which save you time and effort.

- The graphical user interface is easy to understand and use, so you'll be up and running quickly. Once you get started, you'll be surprised at how quickly your "educated guesses" become correct ones.

- All application programs designed for Windows NT look similar: the title bars, menus, icons, even commands are often comparable. In addition, Windows applications use similar keyboard and mouse operations to select objects and choose commands. To a great extent, once you've learned one application, you've learned a part of them all.

- You can integrate with a variety of servers, including NetWare, TCP/IP, Windows NT Server, MS LAN Manager, among others.

- You can take advantage of both 16-bit and 32-bit applications.

- Video and graphics applications run smoothly so that multimedia applications, games, and graphics programs such as CorelDRAW! really shine.

Windows NT's GUI provides a common approach to using a variety of applications for your computer. Learning Windows NT is fast, easy, and fun—and it takes only a minimum of effort.

WHY THE *10 MINUTE GUIDE* TO *WINDOWS NT WORKSTATION 4.0?*

The *10 Minute Guide to Windows NT Workstation 4.0* can save even more of your precious time. Each lesson is designed so that you can complete it in 10 minutes or less, so you'll be up-to-snuff in basic Windows skills quickly.

Although you can jump between lessons, starting at the beginning is a good plan. The bare-bones basics are covered first, and more advanced topics are covered later. Whatever you do, don't miss the inside front and back covers. The inside front cover of this book features instructions for installing Windows on your system. The inside back cover contains a typical Windows NT screen and points out its common elements.

CONVENTIONS USED IN THIS BOOK

To help you move through the lessons easily, I've used the following conventions:

On-screen text	On-screen text appears in bold type.
What you type	Information you type appears in bold color type.
Items you select	Commands, options, and icons you select as well as keys you press appear in color type.

In telling you to choose menu commands, this book uses the format *menu name, menu command*. For example, if I say "choose File, Properties," you are to "open the File menu and select the Properties command."

In addition to these conventions, the *10 Minute Guide to Windows NT Workstation 4.0* uses the following icons to identify helpful information:

Plain English tips define new terms or terms that may be unfamiliar to you, such as technical terminology, jargon, and so on.

Timesaver Tips include keyboard and mouse shortcuts and hints that can save you time and energy.

Panic Button icons identify areas where new users often run into trouble, and offer practical solutions to those problems.

TRADEMARKS

All terms mentioned in this book that are known to be trademarks have been appropriately capitalized. Que cannot attest to the accuracy of this information. Use of a term in this book should not be regarded as affecting the validity of any trademark or service mark.

NAVIGATING THE WINDOWS NT DESKTOP

In this lesson, you'll learn how to start and shut down Windows NT, how to work with the parts of the Windows NT desktop, and how to use a mouse to manipulate items on the desktop.

STARTING WINDOWS NT WORKSTATION

To start Windows NT Workstation, you simply turn your computer and your monitor on. What happens next depends on how your computer is *configured* (set up). The NT Loader screen appears, offering you various options to start the computer. If, for example, your computer is configured for a dual boot, you can select the operating system you want to use for the current session (Windows NT, MS-DOS, or OS/2). If you're using only the Windows NT operating system, you can leave the computer alone and let the default Windows NT operating system start on its own.

 Dual Boot A dual boot is a setup option that allows you to use either the Windows NT Workstation operating system to run your computer, or another operating system such as DOS or OS/2. The NT loader screen presents your options, and you choose one by pressing the up or down arrow on the keyboard and pressing Enter to confirm your choice.

If NT is your only operating system, the computer runs through its general startup and then displays the Windows NT

Workstation *Welcome* screen. Behind the *Welcome* message box, you'll see the NT logo and the blank desktop.

Follow these steps to log onto Windows NT:

1. Press and hold the Ctrl key, then press and hold the Alt key, and finally press the Delete key. Release all three keys, and the second Welcome screen appears.

2. Enter the following information. If you're unsure of any answer, ask your system administrator.

   Username   The name you want to use to log on to the network.

   From   The name of your computer on the network. This box might already have a name in it. If so, enter the name of your workgroup or domain only if the one already there is incorrect.

   Domain   Allows you to select the domain to which you log on. May appear instead of From.

   Password   Your password to get into your computer and onto the network.

Error Message   Many different errors could occur at this point. For example, a message might appear on your screen telling that the connection could not be restored or that you're not a valid user. First, make sure you've typed your password correctly. If you still have a problem connecting to the network, see your system administrator for help.

3. Press Enter to log onto the network. The NT Desktop appears.

Keyboard Shortcut Pressing Enter in a dialog or message box is the same as choosing the OK button; pressing the Escape key is the same as choosing Cancel.

UNDERSTANDING THE WINDOWS NT DESKTOP

After Windows NT is installed on your system, the Windows NT desktop appears each time you start your computer. As you can see in Figure 1.1, the Windows NT screen is made up of many components. These components enable you to open applications, manage files, send and receive mail, and perform many other tasks throughout your work day.

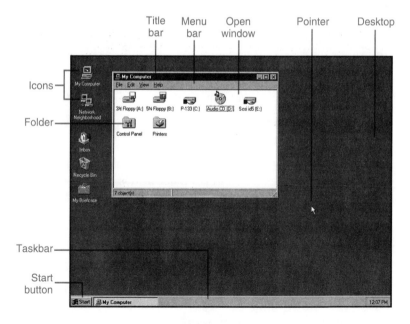

FIGURE 1.1 Common components of the Windows NT screen and an open My Computer window.

The components of the NT screen include:

Desktop   This is the background on which all other elements appear. You can think of the Windows NT desktop like the top of your own traditional office desk. Just as you can move papers around, hide certain items in drawers, and add and remove things on your desk, you can manipulate things on your NT desktop.

My Computer   The My Computer icon represents the contents of your computer, including the hard drive, floppy and CD drives, applications, folders, files, and so on. Double-click an icon to open it and view its contents; the My Computer window in Figure 1.1 shows the contents of the My Computer icon. Double-click any icon in the window to view its contents.

Network Neighborhood   This icon displays other computers connected to your computer either on a Microsoft network such as NT or Windows for Workgroups, or on another network, like Novell NetWare.

Inbox   The Inbox represents Microsoft Exchange, a program you can use to fax and e-mail other computers.

Internet Explorer   If you have access to an Internet Service Provider, you can use the Internet Explorer to access the Net, including Web pages and e-mail.

Recycle Bin   The Recycle Bin is a place in which deleted objects remain until you empty the trash. You can retrieve items—files, programs, pictures, and so on—from the Recycle Bin after you delete them. Once you empty the trash, however, you can no longer retrieve items from the bin.

My Briefcase   My Briefcase is a special feature you can use for copying and transferring files from your computer to a notebook or other computer. My Briefcase enables you to easily transfer and update your files.

Windows   Windows are boxed areas that contain icons representing drives and other hardware, folders (or directories), applications, files, and so on. You can open, close, size, move, and otherwise manipulate windows, as well as add and remove icons from a window.

Title bar   The title bar of any window displays the name of the window. For example, the name of the My Computer window appears in the My Computer title bar. Additionally, the title bar includes three buttons you can use to manipulate the window (you'll learn about them in Lesson 2).

Menu bar   The menu bar contains the menus of commands you choose in order to perform procedures or actions within the Program Manager (or any other application displaying a menu). When you open a menu, a list of related commands appears (see Lesson 3).

Icons   Icons are pictures that represent programs (Microsoft Excel, WordPerfect, and so on), files (documents, spreadsheets, graphics), printer information (setup options, installed fonts), computer information (hard and floppy disk drives), and so on in both Windows NT and Windows applications. Most often, you use icons to open folders, and files (as you'll learn in Lesson 11).

Taskbar   The taskbar contains the Start button, any open application or window buttons, and the time. You can click a taskbar button to open the window or application it represents. Use the Start button to open programs, documents, help, and so on.

Start Button   The Start button displays a menu from which you can choose to open an application, open a document, customize NT, find a file or folder, get help, or shut down the Windows NT program.

Folder   A folder contains files and other folders on your computer; for example, the Printers folder includes icons representing your printer(s) and an application for adding a printer to your system. A folder is the same thing as a directory.

Pointer   The pointer is an on-screen icon (usually an arrow) that represents your mouse, trackball, touchpad, or other selecting device. You use it to select items and choose commands. You move the pointer by moving the mouse or other device across your desk or mouse pad. You'll learn how to use the mouse in the next section.

USING THE MOUSE

You use the mouse to perform many actions in Windows NT and in Windows applications. With the mouse, you can easily select an icon, folder, or window, among many other things. Selecting involves two steps: pointing and clicking. You can also open icons and folders by double-clicking them, and you can move an item by clicking and dragging that particular article.

To *point* to an object (icon, window title bar, and so on), move the mouse across your desk or mouse pad until the on-screen mouse pointer touches the object. You can pick up the mouse and reposition it if you run out of room on your desk. To *click*, point the mouse pointer at the object you want to select, and then press and release the left mouse button. If the object is an icon or window, it becomes highlighted. When following steps in this book, click the left mouse button unless the directions specify otherwise.

The right mouse button can be used when you want to display a shortcut menu. To *right click*, point the mouse pointer at an object—folder, taskbar, desktop, window, and so on—and click the right mouse button. A shortcut menu that presents common commands relating to the object appears. If, for example, you right-click a folder, the menu might offer these commands: Open, Explore, Create Shortcut, and Properties. The items on the menu depend on the object you're right-clicking.

When you *double-click* an item, you point to the item and press and release the left mouse button twice quickly. Double-clicking is often a shortcut to performing a task. For example, you can open a window or folder by double-clicking its icon.

You can use the mouse to move an object (usually a window, dialog box, or icon) to a new position on-screen. You do this by *clicking and dragging* the object. To drag an object to a new location on-screen, point to the object, press and hold the left mouse button, move the mouse to a new location, and release the mouse button. The object moves with the mouse cursor as you drag it.

You can also perform certain actions, such as selecting multiple items or copying items, by performing two additional mouse operations. *Shift+click* means to press and hold the Shift key and then click the left mouse button; *Ctrl+click* means to press and hold the Ctrl key, and then click the left mouse button. The result of either of these actions depends upon where you are in Windows NT.

USING THE START BUTTON

The Windows NT Start button provides access to programs and documents, the help feature, the find feature, and many other elements in NT. You'll use the Start button to perform most tasks in Windows. For more information about using menus, see Lesson 3.

To use the Start button, follow these steps:

1. Point the mouse at the Start button, located on the taskbar, and click the button. The Start menu appears (see Figure 1.2).

2. Click the task or command you want to display, as follows:

   Programs Displays Windows Accessory programs, administrative tools, applications, the Command Prompt program, and so on.

   Documents Displays up to 15 of the most recently opened documents; for quick and easy access, click the document name and the application. The document opens, ready to work.

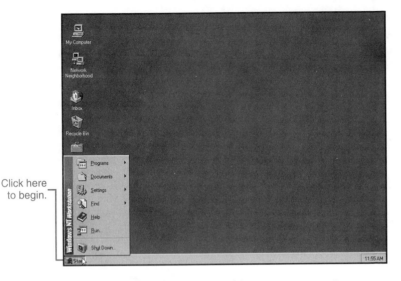

Click here
to begin.

Figure 1.2   The Start menu provides easy access to programs.

Settings   Displays the Control Panel and Printers folders, and the taskbar command for customizing your Windows NT setup. For more information, see Lesson 6.

Find   Enables you to search for specific files, folders, and/or computers. You can search your own hard drive or the network drive.

Help   Displays help for performing tasks and procedures in NT. For more information, see Lesson 5.

Run   Enables you to enter a command line (such as a:\install) to run a program from hard, floppy, or CD disks.

Shut Down   Displays the Shut Down dialog box in which you prepare your computer before turning it off.

Cascading Menu?   An arrow after any menu command means another menu, called a *cascading* or secondary menu, will appear if you choose that command. NT supplies as many layers as four cascading menus starting from the Start menu.

USING THE TASKBAR

In addition to the Start button, the taskbar displays buttons representing open windows and applications. You can quickly switch between open windows by clicking the button on the taskbar. Figure 1.3 shows the taskbar with two buttons: My Computer (representing the open My Computer window) and Exploring (representing the hidden, or minimized, Windows Explorer).

You can move the taskbar to the top, left, or right side of the screen to customize your workspace. Additionally, you can hide the taskbar until you need it.

To move the taskbar, click the mouse anywhere on the bar except on a button and drag the taskbar to the right, the left, or the top of the screen. As you drag, the taskbar relocates to that area. You can easily drag the taskbar back to the bottom if you prefer it there. For help on using menus and dialog boxes, see Lessons 3 and 4.

To hide the taskbar, follow these steps:

1. Choose the Start button.

2. From the Start menu, choose Settings and then choose Taskbar. The Taskbar Properties sheet appears (see Figure 1.3).

3. Choose the Auto Hide check box by clicking that box; then press Enter to close the dialog box. The taskbar slides off the screen.

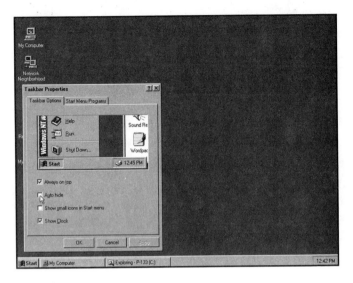

FIGURE 1.3   You can choose to hide the taskbar when you're not using it.

When you need the taskbar, move the mouse to where the taskbar was; you may have to slide the mouse off of the screen. The taskbar reappears.

Show Taskbar   To show the taskbar all of the time, choose Start, Settings, Taskbar and click the Auto Hide check box so no check mark appears. Press Enter to close the dialog box.

SHUTTING DOWN WINDOWS NT

Before you turn off your computer, you must shut down Windows NT to ensure that you don't lose any data or configuration changes. Lesson 26 describes shutting down in more detail and offers various methods you can use. However, to quickly shut down Windows NT, follow these steps:

1. Press and hold the Alt key, and then press and release the F4 key. Release the Alt key. First, the open windows and applications close, one at a time. When all open windows are closed, the Shut Down Windows dialog box appears.

2. Choose Shut down the Computer? by clicking its option.

3. Press the Enter key or choose Yes, and Windows NT begins the process of shutting down. When NT displays a message saying you can safely turn off your computer, you can turn off both the monitor and the computer.

In this lesson, you learned about the parts of the Windows NT desktop and how to use the mouse to manipulate items on the desktop. In the next lesson, you'll learn how to work with windows.

LESSON 2

WORKING WITH A WINDOW

In this lesson, you will learn how to open, resize, move, view, close a window, and how to use scroll bars to view more of a window.

WHAT IS A WINDOW?

A *window* is a boxed area in which you view files, folders, drives, hardware icons, or other elements. Figure 2.1 shows the components that make up a window. Many of these components are the same for all windows in Windows NT and Windows applications, which makes it easy for you to manage your work. Keep in mind that although most windows are similar, you will run across some windows that do not have all of the following components.

You can open and close a window, reduce and enlarge a window, and move a window around—which is what this lesson is all about. In addition, you can open more than one window at a time, stack one window on top of another, and otherwise manipulate windows as explained in Lessons 13 and 14.

Table 2.1 briefly describes the common elements of a window.

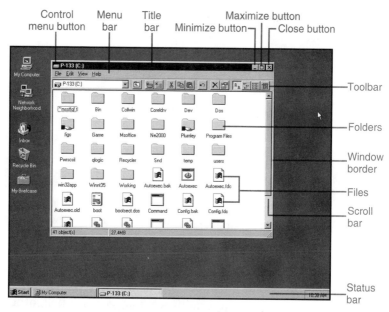

FIGURE 2.1   The elements of a typical window.

TABLE 2.1   **WINDOW ELEMENTS**

ELEMENT	DESCRIPTION
Title bar	Contains the window's name, the Control Menu, and the Minimize, Maximize or Restore, and the Close buttons.
Menu bar	Contains menus with related commands and options that help you control the window and its contents. See additional information about menus in Lesson 3.

continues

TABLE 2.1   CONTINUED

ELEMENT	DESCRIPTION
Control menu button	Contains commands that help you manage the window itself.
Toolbar	Graphic tool buttons that represent shortcuts to various menu commands you use in your work. For more information, see Lesson 3.
Minimize button	A button that reduces the window to a button on the Toolbar.
Maximize button	A button that enlarges the window to fill the screen.
Close button	A button that closes the window.
Folders	Icons within windows that represent directories; folders can hold other folders and files.
Files	Document, spreadsheet, database, program, and other components stored in folders on a drive in your computer.
Window border	A rim around a restored window that you can use to resize the window.
Status bar	A bar across the bottom of the window that describes the contents of the window, such as free space on a drive, number of objects or files in a window, and so on.
Scroll bar	A vertical and/or horizontal bar that enables you to view hidden areas of a window.

No Toolbar or Status bar? If a window doesn't display the toolbar, choose the View menu, Toolbar command; to display the Status bar, choose View, Status Bar.

TIP

WINDOWS CONTENTS

NT is made up of many types of windows that often contain different items. Each icon on your desktop when opened, for example, displays different contents just as various folders, files, and applications display various contents. Additionally, after you open a window you can usually open items within the window, such as icons, folders, programs, and documents. Often, you can open a window within a window within a window, and so on, until your desktop is filled with windows.

Following is an example of a set of windows you can open from the My Computer icon:

My Computer window   Displays hard drive icons, floppy disk and/or CD icons, Control Panel folder (containing icons for customizing NT) and the Printers folder (containing an icon representing your printer).

Hard drive icon   Displays all folders (or directories) on that drive, plus any files found on the root directory (usually C).

Program Files folder   Displays folders representing programs included with Windows NT.

Microsoft Exchange folder   Displays the Microsoft Exchange program file plus other files needed to run the program.

OPENING A WINDOW

To open a window from an icon, double-click the icon. For example, point at the My Computer icon and double-click. If you do it correctly, the My Computer icon opens into the My Computer window.

 Double-Click Trouble? If you have trouble opening a window by double-clicking, you need to practice the double-click movement. You can also change the speed of the double-click to better suit your "trigger" finger; see Lesson 7 for more information.

There is another method you can use to open a window. Just point to the icon and right-click once, and a shortcut menu appears. Select Open from the menu to open the window.

SIZING A WINDOW WITH MAXIMIZE, MINIMIZE, AND RESTORE

You may want to increase the size of a window to see its full contents, or you may want to decrease a window to a button on the Taskbar in order to make room for other windows. One way to resize a window is to use the *Maximize, Minimize,* and *Restore* commands. If you use the mouse, you will use the Maximize, Minimize, and Restore buttons located at the right end of the window's title bar. If you use the keyboard, you can use the Maximize, Minimize, and Restore commands on the Control menu. The buttons and the commands work as described here.

 Select the **Maximize** button, or command, to enlarge the window. A maximized My Computer window, for example, fills your entire screen, thus hiding any of the desktop in the background. Clicking the Maximize button of a program, document, or any other window enlarges it to fill the screen.

Select the **Minimize** button, or command, to reduce the window to a button on the Taskbar.

 Select the **Restore** button, or command,to return a window to the size it was before it was maximized. (The Restore button and command are available only after a window has been maximized; the Restore button replaces the Maximize button in a maximized window.)

Figure 2.2 shows the My Computer window maximized; it fills the entire desktop. At full size, the My Computer window's Restore button is available. When it's any other size, you see the Maximize button instead of the Restore button.

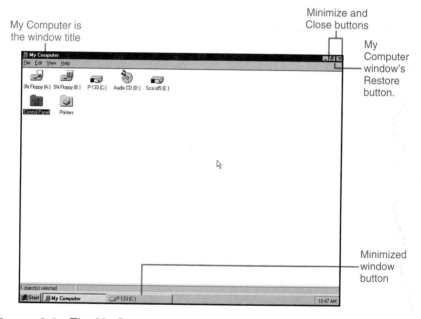

FIGURE 2.2   The My Computer window enlarges to fill the screen.

To maximize, minimize, or restore a window with the mouse, click the appropriate button. To maximize, minimize, or restore a window with the keyboard, follow these steps:

1. Click the Control menu button to open the window's Control menu; alternatively, press Alt+Spacebar.

2. Click the command (Restore, Minimize, or Maximize) you want to initiate. Alternatively, use the down arrow to move to and highlight the command, then press Enter.

SIZING A WINDOW'S BORDERS

At some point, you'll need a window to be a particular size to suit your needs. For example, you might want to fit two or more windows on-screen at the same time. You can drag the window's frame or border to change the size of the window. A window frame appears only on a restored window, not on a maximized or minimized window.

To use the mouse, follow these steps:

1. Place the mouse pointer on the portion of the border that you want to resize. When the mouse pointer is positioned correctly, it changes into one of these three shapes:

 The vertical double-headed arrow appears when you position the mouse pointer over the top or bottom window frame. It enables you to resize the window's height by dragging the frame up or down.

 The horizontal double-headed arrow appears when you position the mouse pointer over the right or left side of the window frame. It enables you to resize the window's width by dragging the frame left or right.

 The diagonal double-headed arrow appears when you position the mouse pointer over any of the four corners of the window border. It enables you to resize the window's height and width proportionally by dragging the corner diagonally.

2. Click and drag the border toward the center of the window to reduce the window, or drag away from the center to enlarge the window.

3. When the border reaches the desired location, release the mouse button.

USING SCROLL BARS

Scroll bars appear along the bottom and/or the right edge of a window when a window contains more text, graphics, or icons than it can display.

Using scroll bars, you can move up, down, left, or right in a window. Figure 2.3 shows an example. Because all of the Hard drive window's contents are not fully visible in the window, the scroll bars are present on the right side and bottom of the window.

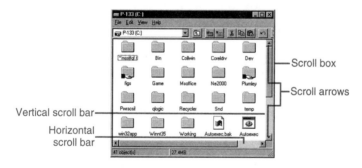

FIGURE 2.3 Use scroll bars to move within the window.

What's a Scroll Bar? A *scroll bar* is a bar that contains three items: two scroll arrows and a scroll box. You use the scroll arrows and the scroll box to move around in the window, scrolling a line at a time, or even a page at a time.

The following steps teach you how to use the scroll bars to view items not visible in the window:

1. To see an object that is down and to the right of the view-able area of the window, point at the down arrow located on the bottom of the vertical scroll bar.

2. Click the arrow, and the window's contents move up.

3. Click the scroll arrow on the right side of the horizontal scroll bar, and the window's contents shift to the left.

By its placement within the scroll bar, the scroll box depicts how much of a window is not visible. If you know approximately where something is in a window, you can drag the scroll box to get there quickly. To drag the scroll box and move quickly to a distant area of the window (top or bottom, left or right), use this technique:

1. Point to the scroll box in the scroll bar and press and hold the left mouse button.

2. Drag the scroll box to the new location.

3. Release the mouse button.

On the other hand, sometimes you may need to move slowly through a window (to scan for a particular icon, for example). You can move through the contents of a window one screen at a time by clicking inside the scroll bar on either side of the scroll box.

Empty Window?   Don't worry if text, graphics, or icons don't appear in a window. Use the scroll bar to bring them into view. Items in any window appear first in the upper left corner.

MOVING A WINDOW

When you start working with multiple windows, moving a window becomes as important as resizing one. For example, you may need to move one or more windows to make room for other work on your desktop, or you may need to move one window to see another window's contents. You can move a window with the mouse or with the keyboard.

 Don't Lose the Title Bar   Be very careful that you do not move a window so far off the screen that you cannot see the title bar. If you lose the title bar, you may never be able to move the window back into full view.

To move a window using the mouse, point at the window's title bar, press and hold the left mouse button, and drag it to a new location.

VIEWING A WINDOW'S CONTENTS

Windows NT displays the contents of a window in icon form; for example, the elements in the My Computer window are represented by pictures of a hard drive, floppy drive, and folders. Other windows, such as your hard drive window, display elements as folders and files.

You can display the contents of any window in various ways so you can better see the contents. The default, or standard, view in most windows is by Large Icons (refer to Figure 2.3). Large icons help you quickly identify the contents. You also can view the contents of a window as follows:

Small Icons   Contents are displayed with a small icon next to the file or folder name; small icons represent the application in which a file was created.

List   Similar to Small Icons but the icons are even smaller than in Small Icon view.

Details   Lists icon, file or folder name, file size, file type, and last date modified. When in Details view, you can click the heading button—Name, Size, Type, or Modified—to automatically sort the contents by that heading. For example, click Name and folders list in alphabetical order followed by file names listed alphabetically.

Figure 2.4 shows four windows, each with a different view of the window's contents: Large Icons, Small Icons, Details, and List.

FIGURE 2.4   Display the contents of a window in a different view so you can easily identify files or folders.

To change views of the window's contents, choose View, and then select Large Icons, Small Icons, List, or Details.

CLOSING A WINDOW

When you're finished working with a window, you should close it. This often helps speed up Windows, conserve memory, and keep your desktop from becoming cluttered.

To close a window with the mouse, follow these steps:

1. Click the Control-menu button to display the Control menu.

2. Click the Close command to close the window.

 Quickie Close   To quickly close a window with the mouse, double-click the Control-menu button.

If you'd rather use the keyboard, select the window you want to close and press Ctrl+F4.

Finally, you can click the Close button in the window's title bar to close it.

In this lesson, you learned how to move, resize, and close windows. In the next lesson, you'll learn how to use menus, commands, and dialog boxes.

LESSON 3

USING MENUS

In this lesson, you learn how to use toolbar buttons, select menus, open menus, choose menu commands, and use menu shortcuts.

USING TOOLBAR BUTTONS

Most windows and applications offer a toolbar containing various buttons you can use as shortcuts. Toolbar buttons represent common commands you often use in Windows, such as cut, copy, undo, and so on. The tools that are available to you depend on the window or application you're using. Figure 3.1 shows the toolbar for the My Computer window.

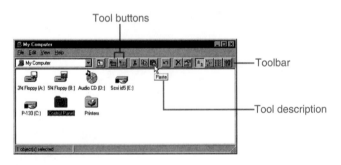

FIGURE 3.1 Use tool buttons to speed up your work.

Handy Helpers Most Windows applications provide helpful descriptors of the tools on a toolbar. Position the mouse pointer over any tool button and wait a second or two. A small bubble or box containing the button's name or a description of its function appears, so you can decide whether to use the button or not.

To use a tool button, click it. Just like commands, any of a variety of results may occur. If, for example, you select a folder or file and choose the Copy tool button, a duplicate of the folder or file moves to the Windows Clipboard for pasting to another area later. If you choose the Undo tool button, the last action you performed is reversed.

WHAT IS A MENU?

A *menu* is a list of related commands that you use to perform tasks in Windows NT and in Windows applications (tasks such as copying or deleting selected items in a window). Menu commands are organized in logical groups. For example, all the commands related to arranging and opening windows are located on the Windows menu. The names of the available menus appear below the Title bar of any window or application that uses menus.

Lost? Any time you're not sure what to do next or how to perform a specific task, click each menu in the application and read each command. Generally, you can find what you want in this way; if not, you can always choose the Help menu (described in Lesson 5).

In this book, I will use the format *menu title, menu command* to tell you to choose a command from a pull-down menu. For example, the sentence "choose File, Properties" means to "open the File menu and select the Properties command."

Pull-Down Menu A menu that appears to "pull-down" from the menu bar. You access the menu by clicking its name in the menu bar. You then have several options to choose from within the pull-down menu.

CHOOSING MENU COMMANDS

To choose a menu command with the mouse, follow these steps:

1. Click the menu title in the menu bar. The menu opens to display the available commands.

2. To choose a particular command, simply click it. For example, to see the View commands available for the My Computer window, click the View menu in the menu bar. The View menu appears (see Figure 3.2).

Click here to display the menu

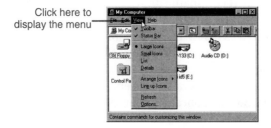

FIGURE 3.2 Click any menu to view its contents.

3. To make the menu disappear, click anywhere outside the menu.

To choose a command on the menu, move the mouse to that command and click. What happens next depends on the menu and command.

Choosing Menu Commands Using the Keyboard

You can also select menus and menu commands with the keyboard. To do so, press Alt to activate the menu bar of the active window. The first menu title is automatically highlighted, indicating that its menu bar is active. With the menu bar active, you can select a menu using either of these two methods:

- Use the arrow keys to highlight the menu title you want, and then press Enter or the down arrow.

- Press the key that corresponds to the underlined letter of the menu. For example, to open the Help menu, press H.

After you open the menu, you select a command from the menu using the same techniques you used to open the menu. Highlight the command using the arrow keys and press Enter, or press the key that corresponds to the underlined letter to select the command you want.

To open the Control menu with the keyboard, press Alt+Spacebar in an application window (such as Microsoft Word), or press Alt+- (hyphen) in a document. Then highlight your selection using the arrow keys and press Enter, or press the key that corresponds to the underlined letter of the command. To close the Control menu (or any menu for that matter), press Esc once to hide the menu and a second time to deselect the menu bar.

 Commands, Options, or Selections?   Commands, menu options, and menu selections all refer to the same thing—items you choose from a menu.

Reading a Menu

Windows menus contain a number of common elements that indicate what will happen when you choose a command, provide a shortcut, or limit your choice of commands. Some menus, for instance, may contain commands that are *dimmed* or grayed-out. However, most commands perform some sort of task when you select them.

Unavailable Commands If a command appears grayed-out, you cannot currently use that command. Grayed-out commands are only available for use under certain circumstances. For example, you cannot choose the Copy command or the Delete command if you have not first selected an object to copy or delete.

Depending on the type of command you select, one of four things will happen:

- An action will take place   For example, choosing File, Delete erases the selected icon or file.

- A dialog box will appear   Any command followed by an ellipsis (...) displays a dialog box containing related options. (See Lesson 4 for more information.)

- A secondary menu will appear   A command followed by an arrow displays a second (cascading) menu offering related commands.

- A feature will be turned on   A check mark or bullet appears to the left of the option you select on the menu, and that option remains active until you either select a different bulleted option in the same menu or deselect the checked option by clicking it a second time.

Separator Lines Commands on most menus are grouped together and divided by separator lines. When (bulleted) option commands are grouped, you can select only one option in the group at a time. When checked commands are grouped, you can choose as many or as few options as you want.

Figure 3.3 shows common menu elements: the ellipsis, the check mark, an option bullet, an arrow with cascading menu, and separator lines.

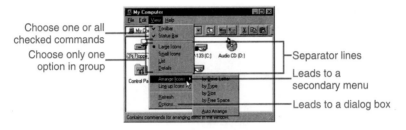

Choose one or all checked commands
Choose only one option in group
Separator lines
Leads to a secondary menu
Leads to a dialog box

FIGURE 3.3 Indicators let you know what will happen before you select the command.

To practice using menu commands, follow these steps:

1. In the My Computer window, choose View, Toolbar. The Toolbar displays, if it was not already displayed.

2. Choose View, Options (notice the ellipsis after the Options command). A dialog box appears.

3. To cancel the dialog box, choose the Cancel button.

USING SHORTCUT KEYS INSTEAD OF MENUS

Until you become familiar with Windows NT and your various Windows applications, you'll need to use the menus to view and select commands. However, after you've worked in Windows for a while, you'll probably want to use shortcut keys for commands you use often. Shortcut keys enable you to select a command without using the menus. Shortcut keys generally combine the Alt, Ctrl, or Shift key with a letter key (such as W). If a shortcut key is available, it is listed on the pull-down menu to the right of the command.

For example, Figure 3.4 shows the Edit menu from the hard drive window on My Computer. As you can see, the shortcut key for Cut is Ctrl+X. You cannot use the shortcut key while the menu is open; you must either choose a command or cancel the menu. You can, however, remember the shortcut key and use it instead of opening the menu the next time you need to cut a file or folder.

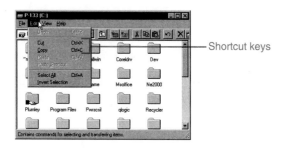

Shortcut keys

FIGURE 3.4   Use shortcut keys to save time.

USING SHORTCUT MENUS

Windows NT supplies a variety of shortcut menus that contain common commands you often use. You can display a shortcut menu by right-clicking an object—the desktop, a window, a folder or file, and so on. The commands a shortcut menu displays depends on the item and its location.

To display and use a shortcut menu, point the mouse at the object you want to explore, open, cut, copy, or otherwise manipulate, and right-click the mouse. The shortcut menu appears; move the mouse to the command and click again. Cancel a shortcut menu by clicking the mouse anywhere besides on the menu.

Figure 3.5 displays a shortcut menu resulting from right-clicking a hard drive icon.

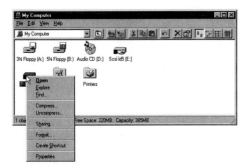

FIGURE 3.5   Quickly access a command with a right-click.

In this lesson, you learned how to use toolbar buttons, open and read a menu, and use shortcuts. In the next lesson, you'll learn to use dialog boxes and all of their components.

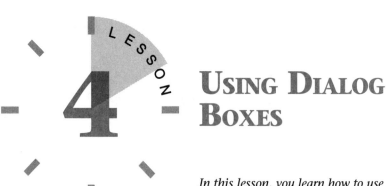

USING DIALOG BOXES

In this lesson, you learn how to use the various dialog box components.

WHAT IS A DIALOG BOX?

Windows NT and Windows applications use *dialog boxes* to exchange information with you. As you learned in Lesson 3, a menu command followed by an ellipsis (...) indicates that a dialog box will appear. A dialog box asks for related information the program needs in order to complete the operation.

What are Property Sheets? Windows NT also uses the term "property sheets" to describe a type of dialog box. A property sheet generally presents information—such as free space on a hard drive, file attributes, and so on—about a selected element in Windows. Property sheets generally supply information and often offer options, just like dialog boxes.

Windows NT also displays dialog boxes to give you information. For example, Windows NT might display a dialog box to warn you about a problem (as in "File already exists, Overwrite?") or to confirm that an operation should take place (to confirm that you want to delete a file, for example).

Box Won't Go Away?   If a dialog box won't go away and your computer beeps at you when you try to continue your work, don't worry. That beep is Windows' way of telling you that you must always respond to a dialog box before you can continue. You can press Enter or choose OK to accept the message or changes in the dialog box, or you can press the Esc key or choose Cancel to cancel the message or the changes in the box.

USING THE COMPONENTS OF A DIALOG BOX

Dialog boxes vary in complexity depending on the program, the procedure, and the number of options in the actual box. Some simply ask you to confirm an operation before it is executed; others ask you to choose, for example, a drive, folder, filename, file type, network path, or numerous other options.

The following list briefly explains the components of a dialog box. Not all dialog boxes contain all components, so don't be afraid to tackle a dialog box.

Text box   A text box provides a place to type an entry, such as a file name, path (drive and directory), font, or measurement.

List box   A list box presents a slate of possible options from which you can choose. Scroll bars often accompany a list box so you can view the items on the list. In addition, a text box is sometimes associated with a list box; you can either choose from the list or type the selection yourself.

Drop-down list box   This box is a single-line list box with a drop-down arrow button to the right of it. When you click the arrow, the drop-down list box opens to display a list of choices. You can often scroll through a drop-down list as you do a list box.

Option buttons   Option buttons present a group of related choices from which you can choose only one. Click the option button you want to select, and all others become deselected.

Check box   A check box enables you to turn an option on or off. You might find a single check box or a group of related check boxes. A check mark appears in the box next to any option that is active (turned on). In a group of check boxes, you can choose none, one, or any number of the options.

Command button   When selected, a command button carries out the command displayed on the button (Open, Help, Quit, Cancel, or OK, for example). If there is an ellipsis on the button (as in Option...), choosing it will open another dialog box.

Tabs   Tabs represent multiple sections, or pages, of a dialog box. Only one tab is displayed at a time, and each tab contains related options. Choosing a tab changes the options that appear in the dialog box.

Using Text Boxes

You use a text box to enter the information that Windows NT or a Windows application needs in order to complete a command. This information is usually a file name or folder name. Figure 4.1 shows a text box and list boxes in the Open dialog box (accessed from the Windows WordPad File menu).

To activate a text box using the mouse, position the mouse over the text box (the mouse pointer changes to an I-beam) and click. The I-beam pointer shape indicates that the area you're pointing to will accept text. Look for the I-beam when you want to enter text in a dialog box. Notice that the insertion point (a flashing vertical line) appears in the active text box.

List box

Drop-down list box

Text box

Figure 4.1   Use text boxes and list boxes to specify your preferences.

- TIP -

Save Time   If you want to replace text that's already in a text box, drag your mouse I-beam over the text (to highlight text) and start typing. When you type the first character, the original text is deleted.

To activate a text box using the keyboard, press Alt+*selection letter*. (The *selection letter* is the underlined letter in a menu, command, or option name.) For example, to activate the File Name text box shown in Figure 4.1, press Alt+N. After you have activated a text box and typed text into it, you can use several keys to edit the text. Table 4.1 outlines these keys.

Table 4.1   Editing Keys for Text Boxes and Other Text

Key	Description
Delete	Deletes the character to the right of the insertion point
Backspace	Erases the character to the left of the insertion point
End	Moves the insertion point to the end of the line

continues

Table 4.1 Continued

Key	Description
Home	Moves the insertion point to the beginning of the line
Arrow keys	Move the insertion point one character in the direction of the arrow
Shift+End	Selects the text from the insertion point to the end of the line
Shift+Home	Selects the text from the insertion point to the beginning of the line
Shift+Arrow key	Selects the next character in the direction of the arrow
Ctrl+C	Copies selected text to the Clipboard
Ctrl+V	Pastes selected text from the Clipboard

 Clipboard   The Clipboard is a tool provided by Windows NT that holds any cut or copied text for you so you can paste it into another location, document, or application. For more information, see Lesson 14.

Using List Boxes

You use a list box to select from multiple available options. For example, you use the Look In list box in the Open dialog box (see Figure 4.1) to select the drive that contains the file you want to open.

To select an item from a list box using the mouse, click the appropriate list item and click OK (or simply double-click the item to be selected). You can also select more than one item in many list boxes by holding the Shift key as you click. In the Files of Type list box, notice that the item you select automatically appears in the linked text box above the list box.

To select an item from a drop-down list box using the mouse, open the list box by clicking the down-arrow, and then click the appropriate list item.

Using Option Buttons

Option buttons enable you to make a single choice from a group of possible command options. For example, the Print Range options displayed in Figure 4.2 enable you to choose which pages of your document you want to print. The active option (the All option in Figure 4.2) has a filled-in circle.

Option buttons ──────────── ────Active selection

Figure 4.2   You can choose only one option in the group.

To select an option button with the mouse, click the circle for the option you want.

Using Check Boxes

For options that you can select (activate) or deselect (deactivate), Windows NT and Windows applications usually provide check boxes. When a check box is selected, an X or a check mark appears in the box, indicating the associated option is active (see Figure 4.3).

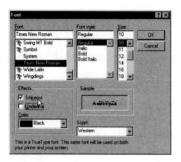

Figure 4.3   Xs indicate the active, or selected, options.

To select or deselect a check box, click its box.

Using Command Buttons

You use command buttons to either accept or reject the changes you've made in a dialog box, to get help, or to access another related dialog box. To select a command button with the mouse, simply click it.

Figure 4.4 shows the two most common command buttons: OK and Cancel. Select the OK command button to accept the information you have entered or to verify an action and close the dialog box. Select the Cancel command button to leave the dialog box without putting into effect the changes you made in the dialog box.

Shortcuts   You can press the Enter key in a dialog box to quickly accept the changes you've made and close the dialog box; similarly, you can press the Esc key to cancel the changes made to a dialog box and to close that box.

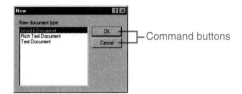

FIGURE 4.4   Use command buttons to control the dialog box.

You can choose the Network command button (found in many of Windows NT's dialog boxes) to access the network to which you're attached. You can access files, folders, and printers from the network or save files to network drives as long as you have permission to do so. For more information, see Lesson 20.

Accidents Happen   If you accidentally select the Cancel command button in a dialog box, don't worry. You can always reenter the dialog box and continue. You need to be more careful when you select OK, however, because the instructions you have entered in the dialog box will be executed.

Close button   Choosing the Close button in a dialog box is the same as canceling it.

USING PROPERTY SHEETS AND TABS

As noted previously, property sheets are similar to dialog boxes in the components they contain: check boxes, list boxes, text boxes, command buttons, and so on. Figure 4.5 shows the Taskbar Properties properties sheet.

Tabs

FIGURE 4.5   Choose a tab that represents the options you want to change.

In a property sheet containing more than one tab, choose options within the sheet and then choose the Apply button to accept those changes. You can then select the other tabs and make any changes you want. Once you've chosen the Apply button, however, you cannot cancel those changes using the Cancel command button. To select a tab, click the tab with the mouse pointer.

In this lesson, you learned to use dialog boxes and their components. In the next lesson, you'll learn to use the Windows NT Help feature.

USING WINDOWS NT HELP

In this lesson, you will learn how to get help, use the Help feature's shortcut buttons, and use the What's This? feature.

GETTING HELP IN WINDOWS NT

Windows NT offers several ways to get online help—instant on-screen help for menu commands, procedures, features, and other items. *Online help* is information that appears in its own window whenever you request it. Windows NT's Help feature offers three help features: an index feature, a find feature, and a contents feature.

The Contents feature displays a list of topics (such as Introducing Windows NT, How To, and Troubleshooting) as well as a Glossary and tips and tricks for using NT. The Index feature enables you to access specific categories of topics—such as adapters, disk configuration, naming disks, and so on. Find lets you search for specific words and phrases—such as About, Checking, Mem, Printing, and so on.

TIP   **Set Up Help**   The first time you choose Find in NT Help, NT runs a Setup Wizard that compiles every work from the Help files into a database you use to find words. Follow directions within the Wizard before using Find.

Fast Help   Most dialog boxes, including Help dialog boxes, include a Help button (a question mark in the title bar) that enables you to get help on items within the dialog box. Click the question mark and point the mouse at an area you have a question about. NT displays a box with a definition or other information relating to your question. When you're finished reading the help, click the mouse to hide the information box.

USING THE CONTENTS FEATURE

You can get help with common procedures using Help's Contents feature. The Contents feature displays the top level groups of information covered in Help, such as How To and Commands. When you select a major group, a list of related topics appears. Figure 5.1 shows the Contents Help window.

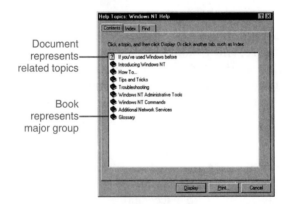

Document represents related topics

Book represents major group

FIGURE 5.1   Choose from the listed topics for task-specific help.

Follow these steps to use Help's Contents feature:

1. Choose the Start button and then choose Help. The Help Topics: Windows NT Help window appears; select the Contents tab if it is not already selected.

Help Tabs   The last tab in the Help Topics window that you accessed is the one that appears the next time you open Help.

2. In the Contents list, double-click the book icon in front of the topic you want to view. The book opens and related topics appear either in a list of books or documents.

3. Double-click a document icon to view information about that topic (see Figure 5.2).

Figure 5.2   A Help window tells you what you need to know when you have trouble printing, for example.

More Help   Anytime you see a small gray button beside a word or phrase in a Help window, you can click the button to see more information related to the topic.

5. When you finish with the Help topic, you can choose one of the following buttons:

Close (X)   To close the Help window and return to the NT Desktop.

Help Topics   To return to the Contents tab of the Help Topics window and select another topic.

Back   To display the previously viewed Help window.

Options   To copy, print, or otherwise set preferences for
the Help windows.

USING THE INDEX FEATURE

Help's Index feature provides a list of Help topics arranged alphabetically on the Index *tab* of the Help Topics window. Either you
can enter a word for which you are searching, or you can scroll
through the list to find the topic. Figure 5.3 shows the Index tab
of the Help Topics: Windows NT Help window.

Tab   Much like a tab on a file folder, a tab is a division
that separates different options in a dialog box. Click a
tab to bring it forward so you can use it.

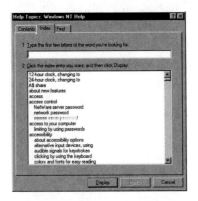

FIGURE 5.3   Use the Index tab to find specific words and phrases
in Help.

To use the Help Index, follow these steps:

1. In the Help Topics window, choose the Index tab.

2. Click in the text box with the number 1 above it and type a topic you want to know about. As you type, Windows moves to the topics beginning with the first letters you enter.

 Browse the List   You can scroll through the index list to see what other topics are available.

3. In the list of topics, select the topic you want to view and choose Display, or simply double-click the topic. The Help topic window appears.

4. When you're finished with the Help topic, you can choose another option, or you can close the Help window by pressing Alt+F4.

USING THE FIND FEATURE

You can search for specific words and phrases in a Help topic instead of searching for a Help topic by category. The first time you use the Find feature, however, you have to instruct Windows to create a list that contains every word from your Help files. (You only have to create the word list once.)

The Find feature is especially useful when you cannot find a particular Help topic in Help Contents or on the Index tab's list of topics.

To use the Find feature, follow these steps:

1. In the Help Topics window, choose the Find tab. If you have used Find before, skip down to the next steps. If you haven't previously set up the Help topics, the Find Setup Wizard dialog box appears. Continue with these steps.

2. In the Wizard dialog box, choose one of the following:

   Minimize Database Size   Creates a short, limited word list.

   Maximize Search Capabilities   Creates a long, detailed word list.

   Customize Search Capabilities   Enables you to create a shorter word list, including only the Help files you want to use. Use this option if you have limited disk space. If you select this option, choose Next, and then choose the topics you want to include.

3. Click the Finish button to create the word list.

When Windows finishes creating the word list, the Find tab contains a text box, a word list, and a topic list as shown in Figure 5.4.

Figure 5.4   Windows now has a word list to search through.

To search for words or a phrase in a Help topic:

1. Type the word or phrase you want to find in the first text box at the top of the dialog box. This enters the word for which you want to search, and Windows displays forms of the word in the word list in the middle of the Find tab.

2. If you see a word that applies to your topic, select that word to narrow your search. If you do not want to narrow the search, move on to Step 3.

Topic List Instead of typing something in the text box, you can scroll through the word list and select the word you want from the list. If you want to find words similar to the words in a Help topic, click the Find Similar button.

3. Click one or more topics in the topic list, and then click the Display button. Windows NT displays the selected Help topic information in a Windows Help window.

4. When you finish with the Help topic, you can close the Help window by pressing Alt+F4. (If, on the other hand, you want to select another option for more information, look at the next section, "Using Help Windows.")

Accidents Happen If you don't want to use the first list that Windows creates, you're not stuck with it. You can rebuild the list to include more words or to exclude words. Simply click the Rebuild button and choose a word list option to recreate the word list.

USING HELP WINDOWS

When you access a Windows Help topic window, a toolbar appears at the top of the Help window and always remains visible. This toolbar includes three buttons: Help Topics, Back, and Options. Table 5.1 describes each button in the toolbar of a Windows Help window as well as the Options menu.

TABLE 5.1   WINDOWS HELP TOOLBAR BUTTONS AND MENU

BUTTON	DESCRIPTION
Help Topics	Opens the Help Topics: Windows NT Help window containing the Contents, Index, and Find tabs.
Back	Displays the previous Help topic window you viewed during the current session.
Options	Displays a menu containing the following commands: Annotate, Copy, Print Topic, Font, Keep Help on Top, and Use System Colors.

The following list describes the Options menu commands in more detail:

Annotate   Enables you to mark any text or topic in a Help window so you can easily find the topic later. A paper clip icon appears beside any annotated text in Help.

Copy   Place a copy of the text in a Help window on the Windows Clipboard for pasting to another document, application, or window.

Print Topic   Send the text in the Help window to the printer for a hard copy.

Font   Select from Small, Normal, or Large type to view the help text; Normal is the default.

Keep Help on Top   Choose whether to always display the Help window on top of all documents and windows so you can easily follow directions as you work.

Use System Colors   Choose this option to restart the Help feature and change the colors in the Help box.

USING THE WHAT'S THIS? FEATURE

The *What's This?* feature provides a handy way for you to get more information about dialog box options. You activate this feature by selecting the ? icon that appears at the right end of the title bar in some (but not all) Windows NT dialog boxes. Figure 5.5 shows a window with the What's This? icon and a description you might see if you clicked that icon.

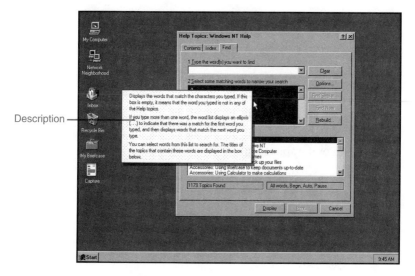

Description

FIGURE 5.5 Use the What's This? feature to get help on certain dialog box elements.

The following steps tell you how to use the What's This? feature to display a description of any option in a Windows NT dialog box.

1. Click the ? icon in the upper-right corner of the Windows NT dialog box. A large question mark appears next to the mouse pointer.

2. Click any option in the dialog box, and Windows NT displays a box containing a short description of the item you selected.

3. When you finish reading the Help information, click anywhere on the screen to close the Help box.

Quick Description   If you right-click an option in a dialog box, a shortcut menu appears displaying one menu command: What's This? Click What's This? to view a description of the option. Note, however, that this only works if the dialog box contains a question mark in its title bar.

In this lesson, you learned how to access and use the features in Windows NT's Help system. In the next lesson, you'll learn how to start and exit applications.

STARTING AND EXITING APPLICATIONS IN WINDOWS NT

In this lesson, you learn how to start and exit an NT application as well as how to view the common elements of Windows NT application's screens.

OPENING AN NT APPLICATION

Windows NT 4.0 provides a Start menu from which you can perform many tasks, including starting Windows programs. To display the Start menu, click the Start button on the Windows Taskbar. You can open the Help feature from the Start menu; you also can open various applications from the Start menu by choosing the Programs command. The menus you see stemming from the Programs menu will vary depending on your system setup (see Figure 6.1).

To open an application, follow these steps:

1. Choose the Start button.

2. Select Programs to display the Programs menu.

3. Choose the application you want to open, if it's listed on the Programs menu; alternatively, select the group containing the application you want to open.

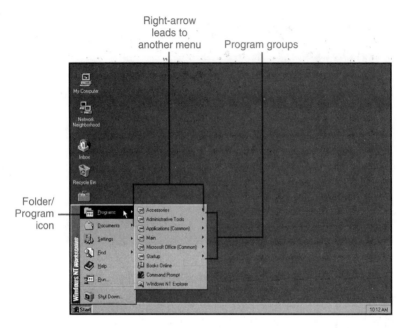

Right-arrow
leads to
another menu   Program groups

Folder/
Program
icon

FIGURE 6.1   Access applications from the Programs menu.

Program Groups   The Programs menu displays various group names—such as Accessories, Administrative Tools, Applications, and so on—that display a menu of related applications when selected. You can identify a program group by the Folder/Program icon in front of it and the right-arrow following the command. Accessories and Administrative Tools are programs installed when you install NT. You may also have program groups for Microsoft Office, Lotus SmartSuite, or other applications you've installed on your computer.

Open Documents   If you have a specific document you want to open that you have recently worked on, you can click the Documents command on the Start menu to display a list; click the document you want to open and the source application opens with the document, ready for you to work on.

VIEWING AN APPLICATION'S SCREEN

Depending on the application you open—whether it's a word processor, database, spreadsheet, or other program—the screen will include elements particular to the tasks and procedures used for that application. For example, the mouse may appear as an I-beam, an arrow, or a cross; the "document" area may appear as a blank sheet of paper or a table with many cells.

Most applications, however, display the following elements: Title bar, Menu bar, Toolbars, Ruler, Scroll bars, a Document area, and a Status bar. Figure 6.2 shows the screen you see when you open Microsoft Word.

Get Help   If you need help with any application, you can click the Help menu and select a Help topic.

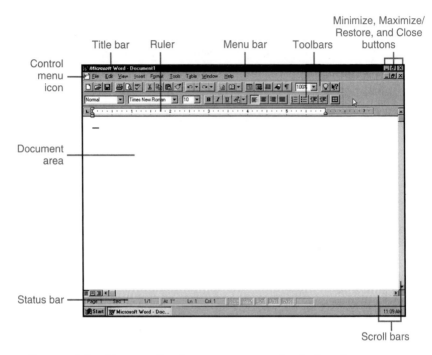

FIGURE 6.2   Most application screens contain similar elements.

Exiting an Application

You should always exit an application when you're done with it to ensure that your documents are saved before shutting Windows down. You can exit most Windows NT applications in one of the following ways:

- Choose the File menu and then select the Exit command.

- Click the Close button (X), located in the upper right corner of the Title bar.

- Choose Close from the Control menu, located in the upper left corner of the Title bar.

- Double-click the application's Control menu icon.

- Press Alt+F4.

Message Before Closing?   If the application displays a message asking if you want to save the document before you can close the program, choose Yes to save, No to close the application without saving the changes, or Cancel to return to the application. If you choose Yes, the application displays the Save As dialog box in which you assign the document a name and location on your computer.

In this lesson, you learned to open and exit a Windows NT application and to view the common elements of application windows. In the next lesson, you'll learn to shut down Windows NT.

SHUTTING DOWN WINDOWS NT

In this lesson, you learn to log off the network and to shut down Windows NT.

LOGGING OFF

You log off Windows NT Workstation anytime you want to restart the computer. In addition, you might need to log off so you can log on using another user account. For example, if you're a member of two or more groups, you might have different access permissions for various resources. Additionally, if more than one person has access to your computer, you log off so another can log on. Therefore, you might have to log off and log back on using another account in order to continue your work.

To log off, follow these steps:

1. Press Ctrl+Alt+Del. The Windows NT Security dialog box appears. In the Logon Information, NT lists who you are, as well as the logon date.

2. Click the Logoff command button to log off the network. The Logoff Windows NT dialog box appears.

3. Click OK. Press Ctrl+Alt+Del to log on as a different user.

As an alternative to displaying the Windows NT Security dialog box, you can log off by choosing Start, Shut Down, and then choosing the Close All Programs and Log On As a Different User option. Choose Yes to confirm your choice. Press Ctrl+Alt+Del to open the Log On dialog box, in which you enter the username and password you want to use to log on to Windows NT.

Ctrl+Alt+Del   In other versions of Windows and in MS-DOS, this key combination warm boots your computer. In Windows NT, however, pressing this key combination when you first start the operating system displays the Password dialog box. If you press Ctrl+Alt+Del when you're already in the program, you see the Windows NT Security dialog box instead.

As you may have noticed, the Windows NT Security dialog box contains a number of other useful command buttons:

Lock Workstation   secures your computer so no one else can access it while you're away from your desk.

Change Password   displays the Change Password dialog box, where you can enter a new password for logging on to your computer.

Task Manager   displays the Task List, which you can use to cancel or end an application that is not responding.

Shutdown   displays the Shutdown Computer dialog box, in which you can choose to either Shutdown or Shutdown and Restart.

Cancel   cancels the dialog box and returns you to the Program Manager.

SHUTTING DOWN THE COMPUTER

You shut down Windows NT when you want to turn your computer off.

Don't Touch that Power Switch   Never turn off your computer with the power switch until after you have shut down Windows NT. If you do, you may lose valuable data or unsaved files.

To shut down Windows NT, follow these steps:

1. From the Desktop, choose Start, Shut Down.

2. When the Shutdown Windows dialog box appears, choose Shut down the Computer, and then choose Yes.

3. Do not turn the computer off until Windows NT displays a message telling you that it is okay to turn off your computer.

 Alternative Shutdown   You can also press Ctrl+Alt+Del and choose the Shutdown button from the Windows NT Security dialog box.

In this lesson, you learned to log off the network and to shut down Windows NT. In the next lesson, you learn to work with multiple windows on-screen at one time.

WORKING WITH MULTIPLE WINDOWS

In this lesson, you learn how to arrange windows, switch between windows in the same application, and switch between applications.

In Windows NT, you can use more than one application at a time, and in each Windows application, you can work with multiple document windows. As you can imagine, opening multiple applications with multiple windows can make your desktop pretty cluttered. That's why it's important that you know how to manipulate and switch between windows. The following sections explain how to do just that.

ARRANGING WINDOWS ON THE DESKTOP

When you have multiple windows open, some windows or parts of windows are inevitably hidden by others, which makes the screen confusing. You can use various commands to arrange your open windows. To access the cascade and tile windows commands, right-click the mouse in any open area of the Taskbar and then select the command from the shortcut menu.

Quick! Clean the Desktop You can minimize all windows by choosing one command to quickly clear the desktop of open windows. Right-click the Taskbar and choose Minimize All Windows. All open windows then become buttons on the Taskbar.

CASCADING WINDOWS

A good way to get control of a confusing desktop is to open the
Taskbar Shortcut menu and choose the Cascade command. When
you choose this command, Windows lays all the open windows
on top of each other so that the title bar of each is visible. Figure
8.1 shows a cascaded window arrangement using WordPad,
Solitaire, and Chat. To access any window that's not on the top,
simply click its title bar. That window then becomes the active
window.

Active Window   The active window is the one in which
you are working. You activate a window by clicking its
title bar or anywhere inside the window, or by clicking
its button on the Taskbar. The active window's title bar
becomes highlighted, and if the windows are cascaded,
the active window comes to the front.

Other open
windows

Active
window

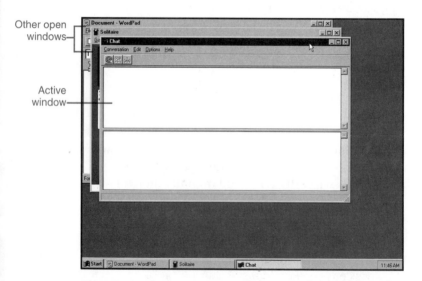

FIGURE 8.1   With cascaded windows, you can easily access the
one you need.

You can still click and drag the title bar of any window to another location on the desktop and you can use the mouse to resize the window borders of any open window.

TILING WINDOWS

If you need to see all open windows at the same time, open the Taskbar shortcut menu and select either the Tile Horizontally or Tile Vertically command. When you choose to Tile, Windows resizes and moves each open window so that they all appear side by side (vertically) or one on top of the other (horizontally), as shown in Figure 8.2.

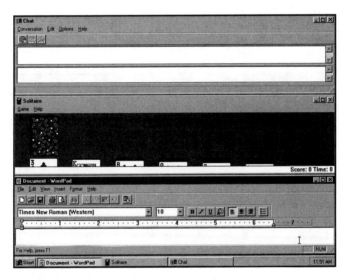

FIGURE 8.2   Tile windows so you can see a part of each window at the same time.

MOVING BETWEEN APPLICATIONS

Windows NT enables you to have multiple applications open at the same time. If the open application windows are not maximized, you might be able to see all of those open windows overlapped, on-screen. In this case you can click any window to bring it forward. Often, however, it's easier to work in a single application by maximizing the application's window. Switching between applications then requires a different procedure. You'll most likely use the Taskbar to switch from application to application by clicking the minimized application button on the Taskbar.

After opening several applications—such as WordPad, Paint, and the Chat feature, for example—you can use the Taskbar by following these steps:

1. On the Taskbar, click the button representing the application you want to open (see Figure 8.3).

2. To switch to another open application, click its button on the Taskbar. The open window minimizes back to the Taskbar and is replaced by the next application you select.

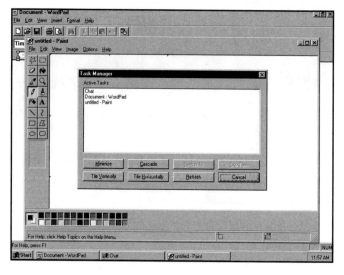

FIGURE 8.3   All open and minimized applications appear on the Taskbar.

MOVING BETWEEN WINDOWS IN THE SAME APPLICATION

In addition to working in multiple applications in Windows NT, you can also open multiple windows within an application. Moving to a new window means you are changing the window that is active. If you are using a mouse, you can move to a window by clicking any part of it. When you do, the title bar becomes highlighted, and that particular window comes to the front so you can work in it.

Figure 8.4 shows multiple document windows open in Microsoft Word. You can switch between the windows, arrange windows, and open and close windows.

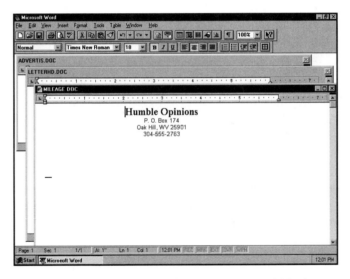

FIGURE 8.4   Three document windows are open within the program.

Open multiple document windows using the File, Open command. By default, each window is maximized within the document area. To switch between open, maximized windows, click the Window menu and select the document from the list at the bottom of the menu. Alternatively, you can press Ctrl+F6 to cycle through the open windows.

To view multiple document windows on-screen, follow these steps:

1. Restore the document window by clicking the document's Restore button. The open document windows cascade in the document area. The Restore button replaces the Maximize button.

2. To activate an open document window, click in the window's title bar or press Ctrl+F6.

3. To tile the windows, choose Window, Arrange All. Windows reduces each open document window and tiles them (horizontally) in the document area.

They're All Just Windows You can use the window frames to resize each window. Likewise, you can minimize, maximize, open, and close the windows as you would any window. (See Lesson 2 for instructions.)

In this lesson, you learned to arrange open windows, switch between application windows, and switch document windows within an application. In the next lesson, you'll learn to copy and move information between windows.

COPYING AND MOVING INFORMATION BETWEEN WINDOWS

In this lesson, you learn about the ClipBook and Clipboard and how to copy and move information between windows.

WHAT ARE THE CLIPBOOK AND THE CLIPBOARD?

One of the handiest features of the Windows NT environment is its capability to copy or move information (text, graphics, and files) from one location to another. This feature enables you to share information between document windows, applications, and other computers on the network.

Windows NT includes a ClipBook Viewer. The ClipBook Viewer contains a window representing your local ClipBook and the Clipboard. The Clipboard temporarily stores data, and the ClipBook permanently stores data that you want to save and share with others on your network.

When you *cut* or *copy* data from an application, it's placed on the Clipboard and it remains there until you cut or copy again. You can *paste* the data from the Clipboard to a document or application. Note, however, that you don't have to open the Clipboard to use it—and 95 percent of the time, you won't. You'll just cut or copy your data, and then paste it to a new location.

Copy, Cut, and Paste When you copy information, the application copies it to the Clipboard without disturbing the original. When you cut information, the application removes it from its original location and places it on the Clipboard. When you paste information, the application inserts the information that's on the Clipboard in the location you specify. (The copy on the Clipboard remains intact, so you can use it again if necessary.)

As I mentioned earlier, data you copy or cut to the Clipboard only remains there until you cut or copy something else. However, you can save data that is stored in the Clipboard by copying it to your Local ClipBook and saving it as a page. At any time, you can add more cut or copied data to additional pages in the ClipBook, creating a saved page that others on the network can use. Figure 9.1 shows the ClipBook Viewer with both the Local ClipBook and the Clipboard windows open. Data that was recently copied appears in the Clipboard window. Saved data appears in the Local ClipBook window.

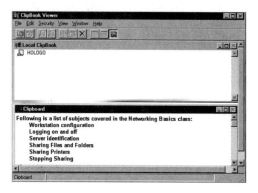

FIGURE 9.1 The ClipBook Viewer.

You can see the contents of the Local ClipBook and the Clipboard at any time by following these steps. (See the following sections in this chapter to find out how to get text into the ClipBook and the Clipboard.)

1. From the Desktop, select Start, Programs, Accessories. Then choose Clipboard Viewer from the Accessories menu. The ClipBook Viewer window opens.

2. Click the Restore button in the Clipboard title bar if the window is minimized in the ClipBook Viewer window. The Clipboard window opens.

3. To close the ClipBook Viewer window, click the Close (X) button.

To save the Clipboard contents as a file, follow these steps:

1. Make the Clipboard window active, and then choose File, Save As.

2. In the File Name text box, enter a file name. You can use long file names if you so desire. Then choose Save.

 Without a Trace   When you turn off your computer or exit Windows NT, the contents of the Clipboard disappear. Be sure to save any Clipboard contents you want to keep to the file.

SELECTING TEXT FOR COPYING OR MOVING

Before you can copy or cut text, you must identify the text by selecting it. Selected text appears in reverse video (highlighted). Figure 9.2 shows selected text in a WordPad document.

To select text with the mouse:

1. Position the mouse pointer just before the first character you want to select.

2. Press and hold the left mouse button, and drag the mouse pointer to the last character you want selected.

3. Release the mouse button, and the selected text is high-lighted.

FIGURE 9.2 You must select text in order to copy or cut it.

TIP **Text Selection Shortcut** To select a single word using the mouse, double-click the word.

To select text with the keyboard:

1. Use the arrow keys to position the insertion point (the blinking vertical line) just before the first character you want to select.

2. Press and hold down the Shift key and use the arrow keys to move the highlight to the last character you want to select.

3. Release all keys, and the selected text appears highlighted.

To cancel any selection (deselect it), click anywhere in the document or press an arrow key.

 Where's My Selected Text? If you press an alphanumeric key (a letter, number, or any other character) while text is highlighted, Windows deletes the selected text and replaces it with the character you typed. Choose Edit, Undo or press Ctrl+Z to reverse the action.

SELECTING GRAPHICS

The procedure for selecting graphics depends on the Windows application you are using. In a word processing program such as Write, you select a graphic by clicking the object. In a program like Paintbrush, however, there are special tools for copying and cutting either rectangular or irregular shapes. Because the procedure varies, you should refer to the instructions for each application.

COPYING INFORMATION BETWEEN WINDOWS

After you select text or graphics, the procedures for copying and pasting are the same in all Windows applications. To copy and paste information between windows of the same application, as well as between windows of different applications, follow these steps:

1. Select the text or graphic to copy.

2. Click the Copy button on the toolbar, or choose Edit Copy. A copy of the selected material is placed on the Clipboard; the original selection remains in place.

3. Click to position the insertion point where you want to insert the selection. You can switch between document windows or between applications.

4. Click the Paste button or choose Edit, Paste. Windows copies the selection from the Clipboard to your document.

TIP   **Multiple Copies** Because the selected item remains on the Clipboard until you copy or cut again, you can paste information from the Clipboard multiple times.

MOVING INFORMATION BETWEEN WINDOWS

After you select text or graphics, the procedures for cutting and pasting are also the same in all Windows applications. To cut and paste information between windows of the same application or windows of different applications, follow these steps:

1. Select the text or graphic to cut.

2. Click the Cut button or choose Edit, Cut. Windows NT removes the selection from its original location and places it on the Clipboard.

3. Click to position the insertion point to where you want to insert the selection. (You may need to open another application or document.)

4. Click the Paste button or choose Edit, Paste. Windows copies the selection from the Clipboard to your document. (A copy remains on the Clipboard until you cut or copy something else.)

USING THE CLIPBOOK TO SHARE DATA

You can use the ClipBook Viewer to share with others on your network the data you have saved in your ClipBook. Additionally, you can access the data in other computers' ClipBook Viewers.

SAVING DATA TO THE CLIPBOOK

Before you can share the data on your Clipboard, you must save the data to your Local ClipBook. To save data from the Clipboard to the Local ClipBook, follow these steps:

1. From the Desktop, select Start, Programs, Accessories. Then choose Clipboard Viewer from the Accessories menu. The ClipBook Viewer window opens.

2. Click the Local ClipBook window to activate it.

3. Choose Edit, Paste, and the Paste dialog box appears.

4. Enter a name for the page and choose the Share Item Now check box (see Figure 9.3).

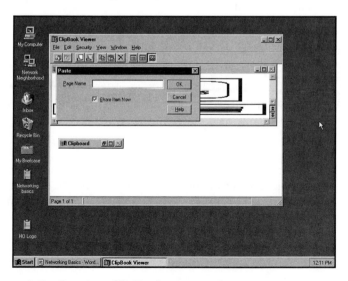

FIGURE 9.3   Create a ClipBook page to share.

5. Choose OK. An icon representing the pasted data appears in the Local ClipBook page, and the Share ClipBook Page dialog box appears.

6. In the Share ClipBook Page dialog box, choose from the following options:

Start Application on Connect   Choose this, and your computer automatically starts the application used to create the shared data when someone tries to access the data. (The application must be running for another user to access formatted data.) You don't need to select this option if the ClipBook contains plain text or a bitmap file.

Run Minimized   If you choose to Start Application on Connect, choose this option so you will not be bothered with the running application as you work.

7. Choose OK to close the dialog box. You can share as many pages as you want by copying the data to the Clipboard and then following these steps to save to the ClipBook.

Accessing Other ClipBook Viewers

You have to connect to a ClipBook on another computer in order to share that computer's ClipBook pages. To copy another computer's ClipBook pages, follow these steps:

1. In your ClipBook Viewer, choose File, Connect. The Select Computer dialog box shown in Figure 9.4 appears.

2. Either select the computer to which you want to connect from the Select Computer list, or type the computer name in the Computer text box if you don't see it in the list.

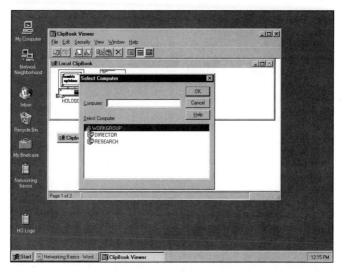

FIGURE 9.4   You connect to another computer to get ClipBook data.

 Two Backslashes?   If you type the name of the computer in the Computer text box, you must start with two backslashes.

3. Choose OK to connect to the other computer's ClipBook Viewer.

4. In the other computer's ClipBook Viewer, select the pages you want to copy and choose Edit, Copy. The pages are copied to your Clipboard.

5. Choose File, Disconnect to return to your ClipBook Viewer.

In this lesson, you learned how to copy and move information between windows and share ClipBook data with other users. In the next lesson, you'll learn how to use the Windows NT Explorer to manage files.

10 LESSON

VIEWING DRIVES, FOLDERS, AND FILES WITH THE WINDOWS EXPLORER

In this lesson, you learn how to use the Windows Explorer to view a disk's contents.

STARTING THE WINDOWS EXPLORER

You use the Explorer to organize, rename, copy, move, delete, share, and otherwise manage your folders (directories) and files. You start the Explorer from the menu. In the Start menu, choose Programs and then choose Windows NT Explorer. The Explorer window opens.

USING THE EXPLORER WINDOW

At the top of the Explorer window, Windows NT gives the name of the drive whose contents you are currently looking at. In addition, the Explorer window is split into two panes. By default, the left pane displays your hard disk and the folders it contains. The right pane displays a list of the files stored in the selected folder. Figure 10.1 shows the Explorer window.

Drive window path   Title bar   Menu bar   Toolbar

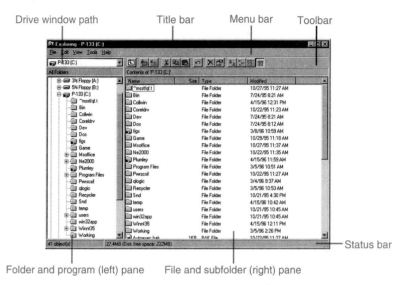

Folder and program (left) pane   File and subfolder (right) pane

Status bar

FIGURE 10.1   Use the Explorer to manage your drives.

Table 10.1 describes the elements in the Explorer window. If you do not see a toolbar or status bar on your screen, open the View menu and select the item you want to display.

TABLE 10.1   EXPLORER WINDOW ELEMENTS

ELEMENT	DESCRIPTION
Title bar	Contains the window name (Exploring), the drive name, a Control Menu, and the Minimize, Maximize, and Close buttons for the Explorer
Menu bar	Displays menus related to disk, folder, file, and network operations
Drive window path	Displays the current path in the window's Title bar

continues

TABLE 10.1   CONTINUED

ELEMENT	DESCRIPTION
Toolbar	Provides various tools for navigating the Explorer
Folder and program pane	Displays the root directory (or drive) and any additional folders on the selected drive
File/Subfolder pane	Displays the contents of the selected folder in the folder window
Status bar	Displays such statistics as free space on drive, number of files in a folder, and so on

Subfolders   A subfolder is a folder within another folder—the same thing as a subdirectory.

TIP   **Folder and File Icons**   Each folder (directory) has a folder icon beside it, and each file has an icon that represents its file type (such as sheets of paper, window boxes, or graphics).

To display drives, folders, and files, follow these steps:

1. In the left pane, scroll the list of drives and folders using the scroll bar. The list displays floppy drives, hard drives, CD drives, the Network Neighborhood, and so on. Select the drive you want to view by clicking it.

2. In the left pane, double-click any folder to display its additional folders in the folder pane. In the right pane, click a folder once to display its contents (files and folders).

VIEWING FOLDERS

Collapsed folders are represented by a plus sign in the folders pane of the Explorer window; expanded folders are represented by a minus sign. Figure 10.2 shows both collapsed and expanded folders.

Collapsed folders

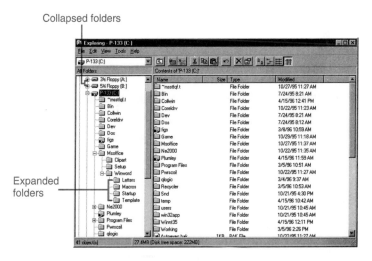

Expanded folders

FIGURE 10.2 Expand a folder to see its contents; collapse it to hide its contents.

To expand a folder so you can view its contents, click the plus sign preceding the folder in the folders pane of the Explorer window.

To collapse a folder to hide its contents, click the **minus sign** preceding the folder.

TIP

Open Folders To open any folder in the right pane of the Explorer, double-click the folder and its contents appear below it in the right pane.

Viewing and Sorting Files

In addition to the file name, you can view various details about the files in a folder: the date created, file type, and file size.

To view file details, simply choose View, Details. Windows displays the file name, type, size, and creation or modification date (see Figure 10.3).

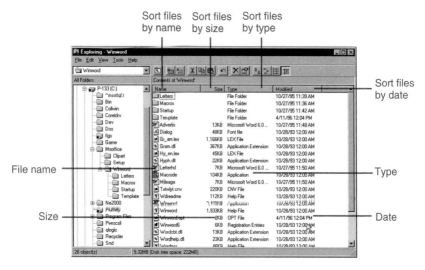

Figure 10.3 You might need to see file details.

You also can use the heading buttons in the files pane to sort the files. To sort files, click one of the heading buttons shown in Figure 10.3 and described here:

Sort files by name Alphabetically sorts files by name, A to Z on the first click and Z to A on the second click.

Sort files by type   Alphabetically sorts files by the file type (Application, Font, Help, and so on), A to Z on the first click and Z to A on the second click. Notice folders come first in the A to Z sort.

Sort files by size   Sorts files by size, largest to smallest on the first click and smallest to largest on the second click.

Sort files by date   Sorts files by date, earliest files created first on the first click and most recently created or modified first on the second click.

 TIP   **Second Sort Method**   You can choose the View menu, Arrange Icons command and choose to sort the files by Name, Type, Size, or Date using the secondary menu.

CLOSING THE EXPLORER

To close the Windows Explorer, choose File, Close, or click the Close button.

In this lesson, you learned how to use the Explorer to examine the contents of a disk. In the next lesson, you'll learn how to create and delete files and folders.

11 CREATING AND DELETING FILES AND FOLDERS

In this lesson, you learn how to create folders, how to delete files and folders, and how to use the Recycle Bin.

CREATING A FOLDER

Many folders are created automatically when you install a program. For example, when you install Word for Windows, the installation program creates a folder on your hard disk and places the Word for Windows files in that folder. You can use an application's designated document folders, or you can create folders yourself. For example, you might create a folder to hold any of the following groups of files:

- Subject-related files (such as all sales documents, whether they are spreadsheet, word processing, or accounting files)

- Application-related files (such as all word processing files or, more specifically, all letters to customers)

- The files for an application that does not create its own folder during installation

- All files you'll share with other network users

To create a folder using the Explorer, follow these steps:

1. From the Desktop, choose Start, Programs, and Windows NT Explorer. The Explorer window opens.

2. In the Drive Window Path on the toolbar, click the drop-down arrow. From the drop-down list, select the drive on which you want to create the new folder.

3. In the left pane, select the folder that you want to be the parent, or root, folder of your new folder.

 Root, Parent Folders   The root folder is the same as the drive. For example, C is the root folder of the hard disk. The root folder is also the parent of all folders on that drive, and any folder is the parent to all folders it contains. (Think of the parent as the drawer holding the file folders.)

4. Choose File, New, Folder, and a new folder appears in the right pane, with the name "New Folder."

5. Type a name for the new folder in the highlighted text box (see Figure 11.1).

6. Press Enter to complete the process.

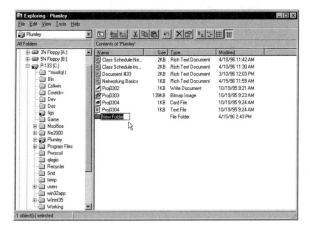

FIGURE 11.1   Add a folder to help organize your work.

Rename a Folder   To rename a folder, select the folder in the Explorer and choose File, Rename. The folder's name appears highlighted in a box; type the new name and press Enter to finish.

DELETING A FILE OR FOLDER

You should delete a file or folder when you no longer need it, when your disk is getting full, or if you created the file or folder by mistake. Before you delete anything, however, it is a good idea to make a backup copy in case you discover a need for it later; make that backup copy to a floppy disk if you're trying to save disk space. See Lesson 18 for directions on how to copy files and folders.

In Windows NT, deleted items are moved to an area called the Recycle Bin and remain there until you empty the bin. Deleting items to the Recycle Bin does not provide any extra disk space. Those items remain on the disk until you empty the Recycle Bin.

To delete a file or folder, follow these steps:

1. In the Explorer, select the file or folder you want to delete by clicking it. You can select multiple files by holding the Ctrl key as you click the files you want to select.

OOPS!   If you delete a parent folder, Windows NT deletes everything in it as well. Be careful to delete only those files and folders you no longer need!

2. Choose File, Delete or press the Delete key. The Delete dialog box appears, asking you to confirm that you want to delete the specified item (see Figure 11.2).

FIGURE 11.2   Delete unwanted files and/or folders.

3. Select Yes, and Windows NT moves the item to the Recycle Bin.

USING THE RECYCLE BIN

The Window NT Recycle Bin holds deleted files and folders until
you empty the bin or recover the files. You can open the Recycle
Bin at any time to view the items in it.

EMPTYING THE BIN

You can empty the Recycle Bin from the NT Explorer or from the
Desktop. You should check the Bin's contents before you empty it
to be sure you're not deleting something you really want. You can
view the Bin from the Explorer.

To view and then empty the Recycle Bin, follow these steps:

1. In the NT Explorer, scroll to the bottom of the left pane
   until you see the Recycle Bin.

2. Double-click the Recycle Bin to display its contents in the
   right pane (see Figure 11.3).

3. To empty the Bin, choose File, Empty Recycle Bin. NT
   displays a Confirmation dialog box.

4. Choose Yes to delete the files.

Deleted Files   Once you empty the Recycle Bin, those
files and/or folders are deleted and cannot be retrieved.

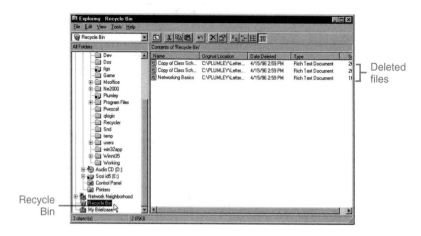

Recycle Bin

Deleted files

Figure 11.3   View the Bin's contents in the Explorer.

Recovering Deleted Files from the Bin

You can move files and folders to the Recycle Bin and then change your mind before deleting them completely from the disk. When you recover a file or folder from the Bin, you're simply moving it back to its original drive and folder.

To recover files in the Recycle Bin, follow these steps:

1. In the Explorer, open the Recycle Bin so you can view the files and folders it contains.

2. Select any files or folders you want to recover and choose File, Restore. NT moves the selected files and folders back to their original place on your hard drive.

In this lesson, you learned how to create folders and delete files and folders. In the next lesson, you'll learn how to move and copy files and folders.

Moving and Copying Files and Folders

In this lesson, you learn how to select multiple files and folders and how to copy and move them.

Selecting Multiple Files or Folders

To speed up operations, you can select multiple files or folders and then perform an action—such as copying, moving, deleting, or printing—on the entire group. For example, you may want to select several files to copy to a disk. Copying them all at once is much faster than copying each file individually. You select multiple files and folders in one of two ways, depending on whether they are *contiguous* or *noncontiguous* in the Explorer window.

Contiguous??? When the files that you want to select are listed next to each other in the Explorer without any files that you don't want in between them, they are contiguous.

Selecting Multiple Contiguous Files or Folders

To select contiguous files or folders with the mouse, follow these steps:

1. In the Explorer, click the first file or folder you want to select, and it becomes highlighted.

> **It's Not Working!**   You cannot select multiple folders in the left pane; you can only select multiple folders listed in the right pane.

2. Hold down the Shift key and click the last file or folder that you want to select. Windows highlights all the items between (and including) the first and last selections. Figure 12.1 shows a selection of contiguous files.

3. To deselect all selected items with the mouse, click any one file or folder. To deselect only one or two items, continue to hold the Shift key, and then click the selected items you want to deselect.

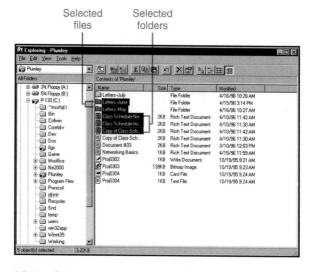

FIGURE 12.1   Select two or more contiguous files or folders by holding the Shift key and clicking the files with the mouse.

SELECTING NONCONTIGUOUS FILES OR FOLDERS

Often, the files or folders you want to select are noncontiguous— separated by several files that you do not want. To select noncontiguous files or folders, you use the Ctrl key.

To select noncontiguous files or folders with the mouse, follow
these steps:

1. Select the first file or folder.

2. Hold down the Ctrl key and click the subsequent files or
   folders you want to select. Each item you click becomes
   highlighted and remains highlighted unless and until
   you deselect the items. Release the Ctrl key when you've
   completed your selection. Figure 12.2 shows a selection of
   multiple noncontiguous files.

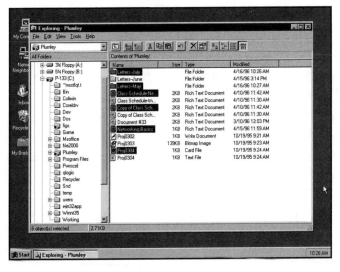

Figure 12.2   Select files that are not in sequence by holding the
Ctrl key when you click.

3. To deselect all selected items with the mouse, click
   any one file or folder. To deselect only one or two items,
   continue to hold the Ctrl key, and then click the selected
   items to deselect them.

TIP   **Selecting All Files**   If you want to select all of the files in the right pane of the Explorer, press Ctrl+A or choose Edit, Select All.

MOVING OR COPYING FILES OR FOLDERS

The time will come when you will want to rearrange files and folders on your system. For example, you might need to move a file from a folder of word processing files to a folder of files related to a particular subject. Or, you might want to copy files you've created into a folder to which certain other users have access. Windows NT provides you with two methods for doing this: menu commands and drag-and-drop.

Before you begin moving or copying files, take these warnings into consideration:

- When you copy or move a folder, you also copy or move the files and other folders within the folder.

- If you move application files to another folder, you may have trouble starting the applications through the Start, Programs menu. Your best bet is to leave application files in their original locations.

USING DRAG-AND-DROP

The easiest way to move or copy files and folders to a new location in the Explorer is to use drag-and-drop. To drag-and-drop, you select the items you want from your source folder, hold down the mouse button, move the mouse to the destination folder, and release the mouse button.

To use the drag-and-drop method of copying or moving files, follow these steps:

1. In the right pane, display the folder or file you want to move or copy.

2. Select the files you want to copy or move.

3. To copy the files, point to any of the selected files, press and hold the Ctrl key, press the mouse button, and drag the files to the folder or drive icon where you want the copy placed.

4. To move the files, point to any of the selected files, press the mouse button, and then drag the files to the folder or drive icon to which you want to move the files.

 Confirm File Replace If you attempt to copy a file or folder to a location in which a file or folder with the same name exists, Windows NT lets you know with a message that displays the selected file's and the original file's size and creation or last modification date. Click Yes to replace the file, or click No to stop the process.

USING THE MENUS

You can use the Copy and Cut commands on the Edit menu. To use the menus to copy or move selected file(s) or folders, follow these steps:

1. Select the files and/or folders you want to move or copy.

2. Open the Edit menu and select Cut or Copy. The selected items are either moved or copied to the Clipboard.

3. In the left pane of the Explorer, select the drive or folder in which you want to move or copy the selected files and/ or folders.

4. Choose the Edit menu and the Paste command. Windows moves or copies the selected file(s) or folder(s) to the new location.

In this lesson, you learned to select multiple files and folders and to copy and move files and folders. In the next lesson, you'll learn how to rename and find files and folders.

13 RENAMING AND FINDING FILES AND FOLDERS

In this lesson, you learn how to rename files and folders and how to find files and folders.

RENAMING FILES OR FOLDERS

You might rename a file or folder to reorganize or to update your work; you might rename files to convert from the old eight-character names to longer, more descriptive ones. The more files and folders you create and use, the more likely it is that you will need to rename them.

To rename a file or folder, follow these steps:

1. In the Explorer, select the file or folder you want to rename.

2. Choose File, Rename. The current name becomes highlighted and appears in a box with the mouse I-beam, as shown in Figure 13.1.

3. Enter the new name for the file or folder.

4. Press Enter. The new name appears beside the file or folder's icon.

But It Worked Yesterday! Never rename program files (most have extensions EXE, COM, PIF, or BAT). Many applications will not work if their files have been renamed. Also, don't rename any files with the .INI or .DLL extensions.

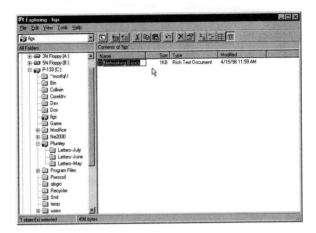

FIGURE 13.1   You can change the name of a file or folder.

SEARCHING FOR A FILE

Using the Windows NT Find program (Start menu, Find, Files and Folders) works similarly to the Explorer's search program. To search for a file, follow these steps:

1. From the Windows Explorer, choose Tools, Find, Files or Folders. The Find dialog box appears with the Name & Location tab open (see Figure 13.2).

2. In the Named text box, type the name of the file or folder you want to find (use wild cards in place of unknown characters).

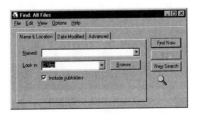

FIGURE 13.2   Tell Windows what to search for and where to begin the search.

Wild Card   A character that fills in for other character(s). When you're not sure of the file name you want to find, you can use the asterisk wild card (*) to replace multiple characters in the actual name, such as *.DOC. You can also use the question mark wild card (?) to replace one character in the file name, such as proj04??.doc.

3.   In the Look In text box, enter the drive and/or folders you want to search. If you enter C:\, for example, Windows NT searches all of drive C. You can, alternatively, choose the Browse button to select the drive or folder you want to search.

Include Subfolders   Make sure this option is checked so Windows NT searches all subfolders within the folders you've specified for the search.

4.   Choose Find Now, and Windows NT searches for the files that meet your criteria. When it finishes the search, you see the results at the bottom of the Find dialog box. Figure 13.3 shows the results of the search C:*.DOC. Notice that the title bar of the Find dialog box includes the search criteria.

5.   When you finish checking out the results, close the Find dialog box.

FIGURE 13.3   The results of the search for DOC files.

In this lesson, you learned how to rename a file or folder and how
to search for a file or folder. In the next lesson, you'll learn to
create and edit a document in WordPad.

14

CREATING A DOCUMENT WITH WORDPAD

In this lesson, you learn to create, edit, format, and save a document in WordPad.

CREATING AND EDITING A DOCUMENT

You can use Windows NT's word processing program called *WordPad* to create a document such as a letter, memo, report, list, or newsletter. Although WordPad is a word processor, it is a very basic application. You cannot check your spelling or grammar in WordPad, there are only a limited number of toolbars and icons to help speed your work, and many of the features are very basic. However, you can create, edit, and format many simple documents with WordPad. Basically, it's fine to use if you don't have another word processor such as Word or Word Pro.

To create a document in WordPad, follow these steps:

1. From the Desktop, choose the Start button, and select Programs, then Accessories.

2. Click the WordPad option at the bottom of the Accessories menu. The program appears with a new, untitled document in the window for you to use, as shown in Figure 14.1.

3. A blinking vertical bar, called the *insertion point*, appears in the upper-left corner of the document area.

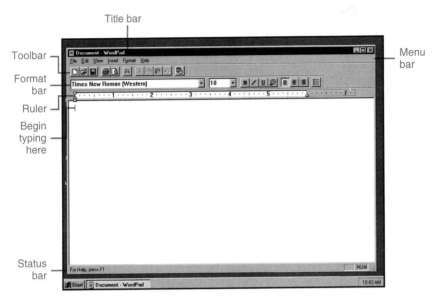

Title bar

Toolbar

Menu bar

Format bar

Ruler

Begin typing here

Status bar

FIGURE 14.1   Use the WordPad program to create documents.

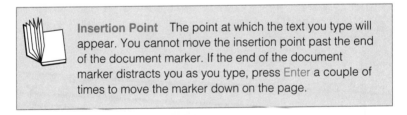

Insertion Point   The point at which the text you type will appear. You cannot move the insertion point past the end of the document marker. If the end of the document marker distracts you as you type, press Enter a couple of times to move the marker down on the page.

Like most word processing programs, WordPad has text-wrapping; you needn't press Enter at the end of each line. Press Enter only to mark the end of a paragraph.

The WordPad screen contains the following elements:

- The Application name (WordPad) and the Document name ("Document" until you assign a name by saving the document) located in the title bar

- The menu bar containing the WordPad menus

- Two toolbars containing shortcuts for saving and formatting your documents

- A ruler that enables you to set tabs and measure margins

- The text insertion point, which marks the location of the text you enter

- A status bar that offers helpful tips and information about the program

Window Elements   Note that the WordPad window contains many elements other windows do: Minimize, Maximize, and Close buttons, a Control Menu button, window border, and so on. For more information about using windows, see Lesson 2.

Need Help?   The Help feature in WordPad works similarly to the Help feature in any window or program. So if you need help, use the Help menu.

MOVING THE TEXT INSERTION POINT

To move the insertion point with the mouse, just click the place in the text you want to move it to. To move the insertion point using the keyboard, see the options in Table 14.1. You can use these keys to move the insertion point around without disturbing existing text.

TABLE 14.1   MOVING THE INSERTION POINT WITH THE KEYBOARD

PRESS	TO MOVE
Down arrow	Down one line
Up arrow	Up one line
Right arrow	Right one character
Left arrow	Left one character
Page Up	Previous screen
Page Down	Next screen
Ctrl+Right arrow	Next word
Ctrl+Left arrow	Previous word
Ctrl+PageUp	Top of screen
Ctrl+PageDown	Bottom of screen
Home	Beginning of line
End	End of line
Ctrl+Home	Beginning of document
Ctrl+End	End of document

INSERTING AND DELETING TEXT

To insert text within existing text, simply place the insertion point in the appropriate location (using the mouse or the keyboard) and begin typing. The existing characters move to the right as you type to make room for the new text.

To delete a single character to the left of the insertion point, press the Backspace key. To delete the character to the right of the insertion point, press the Delete key. To delete larger amounts of text, select the text and press the Delete key (see the next section to find out how to select text).

Selecting, Cutting, Copying, and Pasting Text

Before you can work with text, you must select it. To select text with the mouse, click at the beginning of the text and drag the I-beam pointer over the text so that it appears highlighted. To select text with the keyboard, place the insertion point at the beginning of the text, press and hold the Shift key, and use the techniques described in Table 14.1 to move to the end of the text you want to select. When you release the Shift key, the text you marked appears highlighted.

WordPad uses the Windows NT Clipboard to store cut and copied text until you cut or copy again. To cut and copy text, select the text first and then use the Edit menu. Select the Cut and then the Copy commands. Move the insertion point to the location in which you want to paste the text and then choose Edit, Paste.

Formatting a Document

You can affect the appearance of your document on-screen and on paper by changing the formatting. *Formatting* refers to the appearance of a document, including the font style and size, text alignment, and page layout.

When to Format? You can format text before or after you type it. To format text before you type it, choose the formatting attributes and then enter the text; the formatting continues until you change the formatting again. To format text after you type it, select the text you want to change and then apply the specific formatting changes.

CHANGING FONT, FONT STYLE, AND FONT SIZE

You can change the following text attributes to improve the appearance of your text or to set it apart from other text:

- **Font**   Choose from Arial, Times New Roman, and so on.

- **Font Style**   Apply Bold, Italic, Bold Italic, Underline, Superscript, and Subscript attributes.

- **Font Size**   Choose from 10-point, 12-point, 72-point, and everything in between. (There are approximately 72 points in an inch.)

To change the font, font style, or font size, follow these steps:

1. Select the text to be formatted.

2. Choose Format, Font from the WordPad menu bar. The Font dialog box appears (see Figure 14.2).

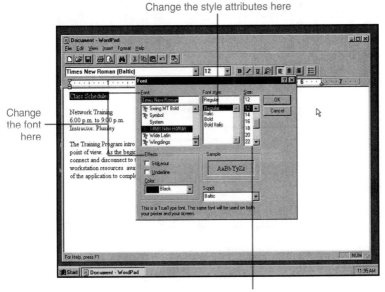

FIGURE 14.2   Change the font, style, and size of the selected text.

3. Select the font, font style, and size options you want. The Sample area shows sample text with the options you selected.

4. Choose OK to apply the font changes.

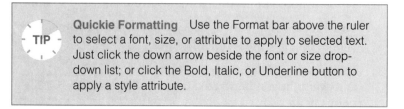

Quickie Formatting   Use the Format bar above the ruler to select a font, size, or attribute to apply to selected text. Just click the down arrow beside the font or size drop-down list; or click the Bold, Italic, or Underline button to apply a style attribute.

Figure 14.3 shows a document with formatting applied to selected text. Note that you can use multiple fonts and font sizes to add interest and emphasis.

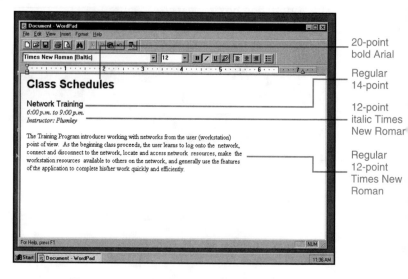

Figure 14.3   You can vary the font, size, and style of text within your document to add emphasis and increase "readability."

TIP **Regular vs. Bold**   A font that has no attribute applied—such as bold, italic, or underlining—is called "regular."

MODIFYING TEXT ALIGNMENT

Normally, text is aligned with the left margin. However, you can right-align text or center it between the margins.

Alignment   Left-aligned text is flush along the left edge of the page and ragged along the right edge. Right-aligned text is the opposite. Centered text is ragged on both the left and right sides, but each line is centered between the two side margins. Justified text makes the text flush with both the left and right edges of the page; however, WordPad doesn't support justified alignment.

To align text, follow these steps:

1. Select the text.

2. Use the formatting bar to choose the alignment: Left, Center, or Right, as shown in Figure 14.4.

ADJUSTING PAGE MARGINS

You can change the page margins using the Page Setup dialog box. You also can choose page size and orientation in this same dialog box.

TIP **Page Settings**   Before you change your paper size, source, or orientation of the page, check your printer documentation to verify it can print to a special setting. Many printers, for example, cannot print to small note paper or A4 envelopes.

Center
aligned

Left
aligned

Right
aligned

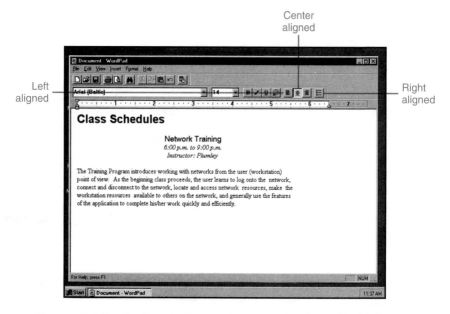

FIGURE 14.4 Centered alignment can emphasize critical information in your document.

To change page margins, follow these steps:

1. Choose File, Page Setup. The Page Setup dialog box appears (see Figure 14.5).

FIGURE 14.5 Change the margins in the Page Setup dialog box.

2. In the Margins area, enter new measurements in the Left, Right, Top, and/or Bottom text boxes. The default measurement is inches.

3. Choose OK to apply the margins to your document.

> **Paper Size** Click the drop-down arrow beside Size in the Paper area to select another size paper, such as a #10 commercial size envelope. You also can choose the paper tray or envelope feeder, if applicable, from the Source drop-down list.

SAVING A DOCUMENT

To keep from losing the changes you've made to your WordPad document file, you need to *save* your work often. The first time you save a document, you assign it a name and location on the disk. After the first time, you can simply save changes to the same named document.

To save a WordPad document, follow these steps:

1. Choose File, Save As. The Save As dialog box (shown in Figure 14.6) appears.

Select a drive here

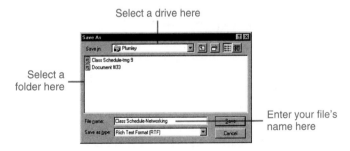

Select a folder here

Enter your file's name here

FIGURE 14.6 Give the file a name and choose a storage location.

Save As or Save? Choose Save As to assign a file name and a location to your document the first time you save it and for any time you want to save the file under a new name or location. Choose Save to save any changes you make to a document that is already named.

2. In the Save In drop-down list, choose a drive to save the file to.

3. In the list box, double-click the folder in which you want to save the file (if you're not saving in the default folder choice). In many cases, you should save to the default folder so you can quickly and easily find the file when you need it.

4. In the File Name text box, enter a name for the file; you can take advantage of Windows NT long file names by entering letters, numbers, and using spaces that exceed the previous DOS eight-letter limitations.

5. Choose Save. Windows NT saves the file, closes the dialog box, and returns to the document on-screen. The name in the title bar changes from "Untitled" to the name you assigned it.

You can also use the File, Save As command to save a copy of your document under a different name or in another location. For example, you might want to create a letter that's similar to one you already have. If you open the existing letter, select File, Save As, and give the copy a different name; you can make changes to the copy. This saves you the time of re-creating the same document.

To exit WordPad, click the Close (X) button or choose File, Exit.

In this lesson, you learned to create and edit a WordPad document, format your document, and save the document. In the next lesson, you'll learn to work with fonts.

Working with Windows Fonts

In this lesson, you learn how to find out which fonts you have, add new fonts, and delete the fonts you no longer need.

FINDING OUT WHICH FONTS YOU HAVE

A *font* is the typeface and style of the type you use in your documents. Some fonts that are available in most Windows applications are Times New Roman, Courier, and Arial. Windows NT supports *TrueType* fonts.

TrueType Fonts   Fonts that are scalable (easily resized) and that look the same in your printed document as they look on-screen. TrueType fonts come with Windows NT and can be used in any of your Windows programs.

In addition to the fonts that come with Windows NT, you may also want to use *printer fonts* that come with your printer software or on cartridges you insert into your printer, or you may want to add fonts from a disk or CD that you purchase from a third-party dealer. Printer fonts may not look the same on-screen as they do when you print your documents.

TIP   **Bitmapped Fonts**   Windows supports fonts other than TrueType fonts. Bitmapped fonts store a unique bitmap (or graphic) image for each font in each size. Bitmapped fonts are formed by small dots, or pixels, whereas TrueType fonts are created from an outline.

The Fonts window (shown in Figure 15.1) contains a list of fonts available on your system. You also can use this window to install fonts to and remove them from your system.

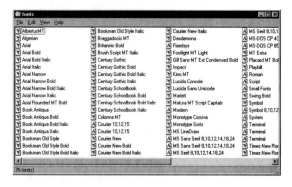

FIGURE 15.1   Use the Fonts window to view the fonts that are on your system.

To see which fonts are installed on your system, follow these steps:

1. From the Desktop, open the Start menu and choose Settings; select the Control Panel. In the Control Panel window, double-click the Fonts folder icon. The Fonts window appears.

2. Scroll through the Installed Fonts list box to see which fonts are installed on your system.

TIP

View Window's Contents   You can change the view of the window's contents by choosing the View menu and selecting Large Icons, List, List Fonts by Similarity, or Details. You also can choose the Hide Variations command from the View menu to hide the bold and italic fonts listings.

3. To view a sample of any of the fonts in the list, double-click the font. A sample of the selected font appears in the Sample box, as shown in Figure 15.2.

FIGURE 15.2   View a typeface in various sizes to see if it's the font you want to use.

4. Choose the Print button to print the font sample. Choose the Done button to close the sample window.

5. When you finish viewing the fonts, you can add or remove a font (as described next), or you can click the Close button in the title bar to close the window.

TIP

Need Hard Disk Space?   If you are running low on hard disk space, you can remove some of your fonts using the Fonts window (as described later in this lesson). To see how much space a font takes, choose View, Details. The size of the font files appear in the detailed list.

INSTALLING FONTS FROM DISK

Because all installed fonts are available for use in all Windows applications, you may find that you want to add fonts to your system. When you add a font to Windows NT, it takes up disk space (however, TrueType fonts take up much less space than bitmapped fonts).

To add fonts, you use the Add Fonts dialog box, which offers you the option of connecting to the Network as a source for font files. To connect to the network, you would choose the Network command button. For more information about connecting to a network, see Lesson 20.

To install fonts from a disk, follow these steps:

1. From the Desktop, open the Control Panel window by choosing Start, Settings, and Control Panel. Double-click the Fonts folder icon. The Fonts window appears.

2. Choose File, Install New Font. The Add Fonts dialog box appears.

3. In the Drives drop-down list, select the drive from which you want to install the fonts (see Figure 15.3). The fonts on the selected drive appear in the List of Fonts box at the top of the Add Fonts dialog box. Alternatively, choose the Network command button and/or the folder in which the font is stored from the Folders list.

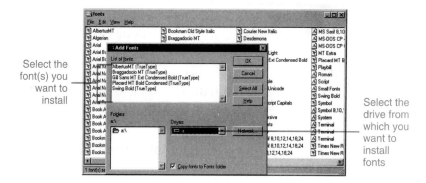

Select the font(s) you want to install

Select the drive from which you want to install fonts

FIGURE 15.3 You can add fonts from a floppy disk, a CD, or a network drive.

4. In the List of Fonts list box, select the font(s) you want to install. To install multiple fonts, press and hold the Ctrl key and click each of the fonts in the list that you want to install. To install all of the fonts in the list box, choose the Select All button.

5. Choose OK, and Windows installs the fonts to the Windows directory (where all the other fonts in your system reside) so they'll be easy to find. Windows returns to the Fonts window, and the newly installed fonts appear highlighted in the Installed Fonts list so you can see them.

6. When you finish, click the Close button in the title bar to close the Fonts window.

DELETING A FONT

Fonts take up space in active memory as well as on your hard disk. There may come a time when you want to delete fonts you don't use from memory and/or from the hard disk. If you decide later that you want to use the deleted fonts, you can always reinstall them using the original program disks. To delete a font, follow these steps:

1. From the Desktop, open the Control Panel window by choosing Start, Settings, Control Panel. Double-click the Fonts folder icon. The Fonts window appears.

2. From the list of fonts, select the font(s) you want to remove. You can hold down the Ctrl key and click multiple fonts if you want to delete more than one font at a time.

3. Choose File, Delete. Windows NT displays the Windows Fonts Folder message box.

4. Choose Yes to delete the fonts or No to cancel the command.

5. In the Fonts window, click the Close button in the title bar to exit the window.

 Important!   Do not remove the MS Sans Serif font from the list of Installed Fonts. Windows NT uses this font for the type in most dialog boxes; if you remove the MS Sans Serif, the text in the boxes will be hard to read. You can reinstall the MS Sans Serif font using the Windows NT Workstation installation disks.

In this lesson, you learned how to view, install, and delete fonts. In the next lesson, you'll learn how to create graphics with Paint, the drawing program that comes with Windows NT.

ADDING GRAPHICS WITH PAINT

LESSON 16

*In this lesson, you learn to open the
Paint program, create a drawing with Paint, and save the drawing.*

OPENING PAINT

Paint allows you to give all of your documents—invoices, letters, reports, and so on—an artistic touch. You can produce simple or complicated drawings to add to your documents, and you can use your creations in other Windows applications such as Word or Word Pro.

To open the Paint program and begin a drawing, follow these steps:

1. From the Desktop, choose the Start button and then Programs, Accessories.

2. Click Paint from the Accessories menu. The Paint window shown in Figure 16.1 appears, ready for you to draw.

In addition to the standard application window parts, the Paint window shown in Figure 16.1 also has a set of drawing tools (called the toolbox) on the left and a color palette at the bottom of the window.

 Outline and Fill Colors The overlapping boxes to the left of the color palette show the currently selected outline color (the box on top and to the left) and fill color (the box below and to the right). The outline color is the color you'll use when you draw lines and outlines for objects, and the fill color is the color of the inside of any objects you draw.

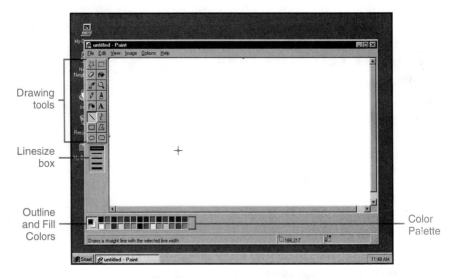

Drawing tools

Linesize box

Outline and Fill Colors

Color Palette

FIGURE 16.1 Use the Paint tools and menus to create a drawing.

The *linesize* box below the toolbar identifies the width of a line and the options for the currently selected tool in the toolbox. Depending on which tool is selected, you might use the linesize box to determine how wide of a line the line tool draws, how wide the eraser is, whether a shape is filled or transparent, and so on. Table 16.1 shows each of the tools in the toolbox.

TABLE 16.1 TOOLS IN THE PAINT TOOLBOX

TOOL	NAME
	Free-Form Select
	Select
	Eraser/Color Eraser
	Fill with Color

continues

TABLE 16.1 CONTINUED

TOOL	NAME
	Pick Color
	Magnifier
	Pencil
	Brush
	Airbrush
	Text
	Line
	Curve
	Rectangle
	Polygon
	Ellipse
	Rounded Rectangle

DRAWING IN PAINT

Drawing is somewhat difficult in Paint, but practice always makes a difference. You use your mouse to draw lines, curves, and shapes, as well as to enter text in Paint.

Follow these steps to draw:

1. To select the fill color, right-click any color in the palette.

2. To select the line color, (left) click any color in the palette.

3. To select the size of the drawing, choose Image, Attributes and enter the Width and Height in the Attributes dialog box (see Figure 16.2). Click OK. The new size is defined by eight small black handles, or boxes, outlining the specified area.

4. Click a drawing tool in the toolbox at the left of the screen.

FIGURE 16.2   Choose the size of the drawing before you begin drawing.

 TIP   **Which Tool?**   Try starting with either the rectangle tool, the ellipse tool, or the straight line tool to experiment. Then branch out to the other tools as you learn more about the program.

---

5. To select a line width for any line tool—line, curve, rectangle, ellipse, and so on—click the line size you want in the linesize box in the lower-left corner of the screen.

6. To draw an object, point at the area where you want the object to appear (within the boxed Image area), press and hold the left mouse button, and drag the mouse pointer until the object is the size you want.

Oops! If you add to your graphic and then decide you don't like the addition, choose Edit, Undo (or press Ctrl+Z) to undo the change you made.

A Perfect Circle Every Time To draw a perfect circle, select the Ellipse tool, hold down the Shift key, and click and drag the mouse pointer. You can also use this technique to draw a perfect square with the Rectangle tool or a perfectly straight line with the Line tool.

ADDING TEXT TO A GRAPHIC

Using the Text tool, you can add text to a graphic such as a logo. To add text to a graphic, follow these steps:

1. Select the Text tool.

2. Drag the text tool to create a rectangle in which you will type the text. A rectangle that will hold the text and an insertion point appear.

3. Before you type, choose View, Text Toolbar. The Fonts toolbar appears, as shown in Figure 16.3. Choose the font, size, and attributes from the Fonts toolbar.

4. Click the insertion point within the rectangle and type your text, pressing Enter at the end of each line. When you finish typing the text, choose another tool from the toolbox or click the next place you want to insert a new line of text. If you want to make a change to the formatting of the text, select the text and use the Font toolbar to make any changes.

5. Click outside of the text box anywhere to accept the text you just entered.

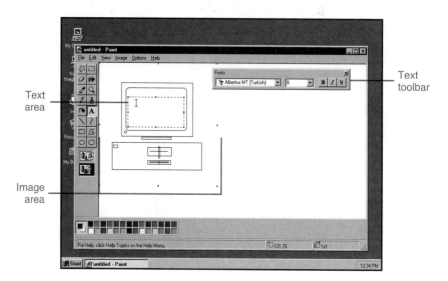

Text toolbar

Text area

Image area

FIGURE 16.3 Use Paint's tools to create a company logo.

Once You Leave, You Can Never Get Back You can't edit or reformat text once you've accepted it; you can only erase it. To erase the text, click the Select tool, draw a frame around the text, and choose Edit, Cut. (This also works for any lines or shapes you draw.) Be careful when cutting, however; you can cut out parts of shapes and text and leave other parts there.

TIP **Move or Size Object** To move the text (or any other part of the drawing), select it with the Select tool and then drag it to a new position. To resize an object, select it and then position the mouse pointer over one of the handles around the selection rectangle. Drag the two-headed arrow to change the size of the text or object.

Figure 16.4 shows a logo using graphics and text created in Paint, with the text selected and ready to move.

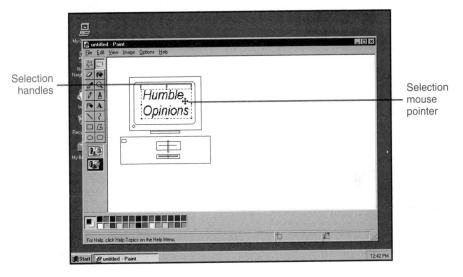

Selection handles

Selection mouse pointer

FIGURE 16.4   Create a company logo.

SAVING THE DRAWING

Most likely, you will want to save your drawing so that you can use it over again; you might want to use it in a WordPad document, for example. For more information about sharing information between Windows programs, see Lesson 14.

To save a drawing, follow these steps:

1. Choose File, Save As. The Save As dialog box appears.

2. If you want to change the file type, choose a file type from the Save as Type drop-down list box.

3. In the Save In drop-down list box, choose a drive in which to save the file.

4. In the list box, double-click the folder to which you want to save the file.

5. In the File Name box, enter a name for the file. Choose
   Save, and Paint saves the file.

6. To close Paint, click the Close button or choose File, Exit.

 Want to Print It?   To learn how to print in Windows
programs, see Lesson 11.

In this lesson, you learned to use the Windows Paint accessory
program. In the next lesson, you'll learn to print from
Windows NT.

PRINTING WITH WINDOWS NT

In this lesson, you learn to print from an application, control the print job, and connect to a network printer.

PRINTING FROM AN APPLICATION

The steps for printing from any Windows application are very similar. The biggest difference is that some dialog box options change from program to program. Most programs offer a Print icon on the toolbar that you can click to print one copy of the job; although in some programs, the print icon displays the Print dialog box. To print from a Windows application, follow these steps:

1. Choose File, Print, and the Print dialog box appears. Figure 17.1 shows the Print dialog box in the WordPad accessory program.

FIGURE 17.1 Use the Print dialog box to specify printing options.

2. Set any of the printing options described in the following list. (Some applications will offer more specialized options; see a particular application's Help feature if you have questions.)

Print Range   Specify the pages you want to print. For example, you can print all pages, the current page, a range of pages (list the pages in the provided text box), or a selection (which you select before opening the Print dialog box).

Copies   Enter the number of copies to print. Often, you can choose a print order (front to back, for example) and whether to collate the copies or not.

Print to File   Prints the document into a file, which you can use to print your document from a computer that doesn't have the program you used to create it. (You then print the file by typing **print** *filename* at the DOS prompt of any computer. All document formatting is preserved.)

Printer   If you have several printers available, you can choose the printer to which you want to send the job.

Properties or **Setup**   Usually leads to a dialog box in which you can set paper size, orientation, paper tray, graphics resolution, and other options specific to your printer.

3. When you're ready to print, choose OK. Windows NT sends the job to the printer.

Printing Errors   If your job doesn't print and you receive an error message from Windows NT, write the message down so you can ask your system administrator about it. Before you do that, though, make sure that the printer is on and there is paper in it.

Print Job   A print job is a document you are printing. Each time you choose OK in the Print dialog box, you are sending a print job to the printer (whether that document contains one page or forty pages).

WORKING WITH THE PRINT FOLDER

When you print a document, the printer usually begins processing the job immediately. But what if the printer is working on
another job that you (or someone else, if you're working on a
network printer) sent? When that happens, there is a print queue
that holds the job until the printer is ready for it.

Print Queue A holding area for jobs waiting to be
printed. If you were to open the contents of the queue,
the jobs would appear in the order they were sent to the
printer.

You can check on the status of a print job you've sent by looking
at the Print queue, found in the Printers folder. Figure 17.2 shows
a document in the Print queue. As you can see, the print queue
window displays the information about the job. In this figure, the
status shows that the printer is offline. If the printer were online,
"Printing" would appear in the status column.

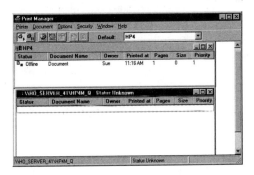

FIGURE 17.2   Use the Print queue to track your print jobs.

To display the Print queue, follow these steps:

1. From the Desktop, choose the Start button and then
   choose Settings, and Printers.

2. In the Printers folder, double-click the printer to which
   you are printing.

Empty Print Queue?   If no jobs appear in the Print queue, the job has already been sent to the printer.

CONTROLLING THE PRINT JOB

It's hard to control just one or two jobs because they usually go to the printer too quickly. However, if there are several jobs in the queue, you can control them. For example, you can pause and resume print jobs, and you can delete a job before it prints.

To be completely fair to other users, Windows will not let you mess with other people's print jobs. If you share a network printer, you can control only your own print jobs (unless you have full control access).

Full Control Access   The system administrator sets printer permissions that specify the access each user has to that printer. A user with Full Control permission can completely control the print jobs. He or she can modify print settings, printer properties, and users of the printer; pause, resume, and delete a job; and change the order of the print jobs.

PAUSING AND RESUMING THE PRINT QUEUE

You may want to pause the queue and then resume printing later if, for example, the paper in the printer is misaligned or the printer is using the wrong color paper. Pausing the print queue gives you time to correct the problem. To pause the print queue, choose Printer, Pause Printing. To resume printing, choose Printer, Pause Printing a second time to remove the check mark beside the command.

Printer Stalled If your printer stalls while it's processing your print job, Windows displays the word "stalled" in the printer status line. Choose Printer, Pause Printing to remove the check mark from the command and start printing again. If the printer stalls again, see if there's a problem with the printer (it might be offline or out of paper, for example).

DELETING A PRINT JOB

Sometimes you'll send a document to be printed and then change your mind. For example, you may think of additional text to add to the document or realize you forgot to spell-check your work. In such a case, deleting the print job is easy. Follow these steps:

1. Open the Print queue by choosing Start, Settings, and Printers; double-click the printer.

2. Click the job you want to delete.

3. Choose Document, Cancel.

 Clear the Queue! To remove all the files from the print queue, choose Printer, Purge Print Documents. Note, however, that this removes only your own documents from the print queue (unless you have Full Control permission).

INSTALLING A NETWORK PRINTER

You can install a network printer to your hard drive so you can easily print without going through the steps of connecting to the network printer. When you install a network printer, you add it to your Printers folder and, therefore, to your printers list in any Print dialog box. When you're ready to print, you choose the network printer from the Print dialog box.

To install a network printer, follow these steps:

1. From the Desktop, choose Start, Settings, Printers. The Printers window opens, displaying the printers attached to your computer.

2. Double-click the Add Printer icon in the Printers window. The first screen of the Add Printer Wizard appears as shown in Figure 17.3.

FIGURE 17.3   Add a network printer to your list of printers.

3. Choose the Network Printer Server option and choose the Next button. Follow the directions on-screen to complete installation.

To print from the network printer in any application, choose File, Print. In the Printers area of the Print dialog box, select the printer from the server as the current printer. Choose OK.

In this lesson, you learned how to print from an application, control print jobs, and connect to and install a network printer. In the next lesson, you'll learn how to view a network drive.

VIEWING A NETWORK DRIVE

In this lesson, you learn to connect to the network,
to log on as a different user, and to display shared files on the network.

UNDERSTANDING THE NETWORK

You can use Windows NT Workstation with a number of network server systems, including Novell NetWare, systems that use TCP/IP, Windows NT Server, Microsoft LAN Manager, and IBM LAN Server. Most networks consist of servers and clients, although some networks consist solely of workstations (called "peer-to-peer" networks). Windows NT Workstation is a client that can attach and share data with various servers and with a peer-to-peer network. When you connect to a network, you gain certain advantages:

- Access to shared resources, such as files and printers

- Access to shared data, such as ClipBook pages

- The capability to send and receive messages with others on the network using a mail program

- The capability to back up your files to the server (see your system administrator for more information)

System Administrator   The system or network administrator is the person who oversees your network. The administrator can grant a user permission to access certain files and resources, troubleshoot problems with the network, and control each computer on the network.

Client/Server   A client/server network is one in which the NT workstation logs on to and attaches to a server that controls shared files, printers, and other resources. Examples of client/server networks include NetWare and Windows NT Server.

Peer-to-peer   A peer-to-peer network is one in which all workstations are connected and each can share its printer, files, folders, and other resources. Examples of peer-to-peer networks include Windows (3.11) for Workgroups, Windows NT Workstation, and Windows 95 network.

Using a User Name and Password

You know that to gain access to Windows NT, you must enter your user name and password, which identify you to the computer, and to the network, if you are attached to one. The user name that appears when you log on to Windows NT and the password you enter are those that you or the system administrator created while running Setup. These devices provide security not only for your work, but for the entire network. Therefore, someone who does not know his or her user name and password cannot log on to the network.

After you do log on, you can run applications, print and save files, share files, and so on. You also have control over who shares the files and directories on your computer (see Lessons 21 and 22).

Log On To connect to a network, you must log on. When you log on, you're essentially telling the network that you're ready to share its resources. The network uses your logon as a key, of sorts, to identify which resources you may use.

ACCESSING SHARED RESOURCES

Your system administrator grants you and everyone on the network certain rights that control which network files and resources you can access. Most of the people on the network have a user account just as you do, which means you all generally share the same resources.

CONNECTING TO A NETWORK DRIVE

When you connect to a network drive, you add a whole new set of folders, and files—not to mention other resources—to your working environment. After connecting, you can remain connected to the network while you work, or if you need to access something else, you can disconnect from the network and connect again at any time. (You might disconnect from one server to attach to another server, for example, or disconnect from one network to connect to another.)

To connect to the network, follow these steps:

1. From the Desktop, double-click the Network Neighborhood to open that window. Figure 18.1 shows the Network Neighborhood window displaying a peer-to-peer Windows network. Depending on the network you're attached to, your Network Neighborhood window may look different, but the theory and procedure are the same.

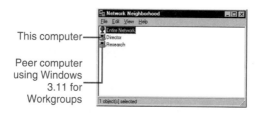

This computer

Peer computer
using Windows
3.11 for
Workgroups

Figure 18.1 You can access any available network and connect to multiple networks.

2. If you do not see your network in the Network Neighborhood window, double-click the Entire Network icon. The Entire Network window opens, displaying the networks and/or domains available to you.

3. Double-click the appropriate network (if you're unsure, see your system administrator), and the appropriate domain if applicable, to display the computers, printers, or servers you want to access.

4. To attach to a computer on a peer-to-peer network or to a server, double-click that computer's icon in the Network window. A list of files, folders, printers, and/or other shared resources appears. Figure 18.2 shows the stepped windows to open to access the folders on a NetWare server.

Don't Panic! If you cannot access a network drive, don't worry. The server might be down for repair, a cable might have become loose, your permission rights might have expired, or some other problem might have occurred. All of these are problems that can be easily solved by—you guessed it—your system administrator. Report the problem and be patient.

Double-click Entire Network   Double-click NetWare

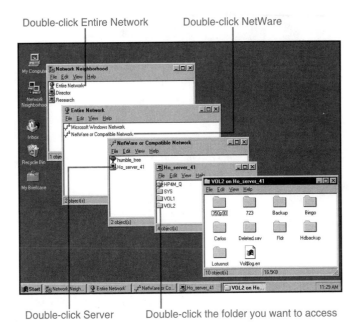

Double-click Server   Double-click the folder you want to access

Figure 18.2   Continue to open windows until you find the folder, file, printer, or other resource you want.

Displaying Files

You can display files on the network drive in either the Network Neighborhood or the Explorer; either way, you can treat the files and folders just as you would any files on your own hard drive, as long as you've been granted permissions and rights. In the All Folders window, double-click any folder to display its contents. And don't forget that you can use the View menu to display the files by Detail; then you can sort the files by name, type, size, and/or date. (See Lesson 2 for more information on viewing a window's contents.)

In this chapter, you learned to connect to a network drive and to log on as a different user. You also learned how to view files on the network. In the next lesson, you'll learn to share folders and printers, change sharing properties, and view shared files.

19 LESSON SHARING FOLDERS AND FILES

In this lesson, you learn to share folders and printers, change sharing properties, view shared files, and stop sharing resources.

UNDERSTANDING GROUP MEMBERSHIPS

Windows NT creates several groups of users within the workstation and the network, including Administrators, Power Users, Users, Guests, Backup Operators, and special groups. Each group has certain access rights on the network. For example, the Guests group has very limited access to resources, files, printers, and so on within the network.

The system administrator assigns each person on the network to a group, thus granting that person certain access rights assigned to the group. The following list describes each group and its network access rights:

- **Administrators**   The most powerful group, administrators manage the overall configuration of the workstations and access to most workstation resources.

- **Power Users**   Power users have limited access to the users' accounts. A power user can share folders on the network, install and share printers, and create program groups.

- **Users**   Members of the Users group can perform every-day tasks with their computers; they can run applications, save and print files, customize their own setup, and so on.

- **Database**   Members collect and compile data about the network use and members.

- **Replicator**   Members support file replication in a domain.

- **Guests**   Guests are often limited to one-time access, which enables them to log on and view limited areas of the network.

- **Backup Operators**   The backup operators back up and restore folders and files; therefore, they have the access rights to workstations' files for this purpose.

Of course, the system administrator has the authority to create other groups for specific purposes.

SHARING A FOLDER

During setup, Windows NT automatically designates one folder (usually named WINNT) as a shared folder. This folder contains your Windows NT files, as well as other pertinent information about your system. The Administrators and Backup Operator groups can access this folder through the network at any time, but they are the only individuals who can access this folder.

You can designate other folders on your computer as "shared" so that others on the network can view and use them. All files within a shared folder are also shared, unless you specifically mark some as not shared (as described in Lesson 22). Each shared folder has an outstretched hand icon next to it in the Explorer's window (see Figure 19.1).

To share a folder, you must be logged on as a member of the Administrators or Power Users group. Follow these steps to mark a folder for sharing:

1. In the Explorer's All Folders window, select the folder you want to share.

2. Choose File, Properties. That folder's Properties dialog box appears.

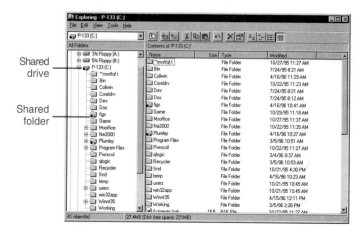

Shared
drive

Shared
folder

FIGURE 19.1   The hand icon designates a shared folder.

3. Choose the Sharing tab and select the Shared As option
   (see Figure 19.2).

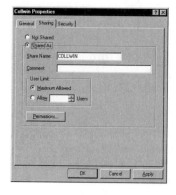

FIGURE 19.2   Choose to share a folder and then set limits on who
can share it.

4. Fill in the following text boxes:

> Share Name   Enter the name a user will specify when
> he or she wants to connect to the shared folder. (By
> default, this is the name of the selected folder.)

> Comment   (Optional) Enter a note to describe the
> folder.

Permissions Permissions deal with specific rights granted to each group. For more information, see Lesson 22.

5. In the User Limit area, indicate the maximum number of users who can connect to the folder at one time; you might want to set a limit, for example, to cut down on network traffic. Select Maximum Allowed if you don't want to set a limit; select Allow and fill in the maximum number if you do want to set a limit.

6. Choose OK to share the folder and close the dialog box. The outstretched hand icon now appears next to the selected folder in the Explorer folder window.

SHARING A PRINTER

When you share your printer, you're enabling others on the network to connect to your printer and print their own documents. You designate a shared printer in the Printers folder.

Your Printer You can only control sharing a printer with another printer that's directly connected to your computer. You cannot control a printer connected to another computer or a network printer.

To share a printer, follow these steps:

1. In the Explorer, open the Printers window by double-clicking the Printers folder in the left pane. A list of printers appears in the right pane.

2. Select the printer attached to your computer (local printer) and choose File, Properties. The printer's Properties dialog box appears.

3. Choose the Sharing tab and select the Shared option button (see Figure 19.3).

Printers folder

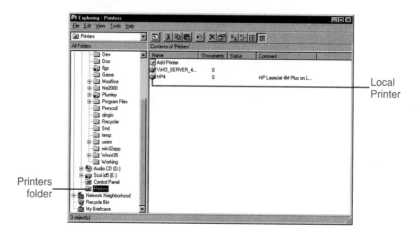

Local Printer

Figure 19.3   Choose to share in the Properties dialog box.

4. In the Share Name text box, enter a name to represent the printer to other users, if you want, and choose OK.

Changing Sharing Properties

Sharing properties include the number of users allowed to connect to a shared folder and the comment information. You can change these sharing properties at any time, as long as you are logged on to the network as a member of the Administrators or Power Users group. To change sharing properties for folders, follow these steps:

1. In the left pane of the Explorer, select the shared folder for which you want to change properties.

2. Choose File, Properties. The folder's Properties dialog box appears.

3. Choose the Sharing tab and change any of the following sharing properties for the selected folder:

- In the Comment text box, enter a new description or replace the current one.

- In the User Limit area, change the option for the maximum number of users allowed to access the selected folder.

- Choose the New Share button to assign another share name to the folder. In the New Share dialog box, enter a new share name and comment, apply a user limit, and click OK. The dialog box closes, and Windows adds the new share name to the Shared Folder dialog box.

4. Click OK to close the dialog box and put the changes into effect.

SHARING FILES

You can select individual files on your computer and choose whether or not to share the files. You can also determine to what degree you want to share by setting file attributes. Attributes are file markers that indicate information about the file. You can assign the following attributes to a file:

- **Read-Only**   Enables others to view the file, but prevents them from changing the file's contents or saving it.

- **Hidden**   Hides the file so that it is not listed in the folder. However, you can still access it if you know it's there.

- **Archive**   Marks a file for backup.

- **System**   Indicates specific files that Windows NT and the computer need to run.

- **Compressed**   Marks files that Windows has shrunk (compressed files take up less space in your computer's memory).

The system assigns many file attributes in order to protect the file or identify it to the system. However, you can also assign attributes to your files to protect them.

 You're Limited When Setting Attributes If your system uses the Windows NT file system (NTFS), you must have permission to change file attributes. See your system administrator.

To set file attributes, follow these steps:

1. In the Explorer, select the file you want to share.

2. Choose File, Properties. The file's Properties dialog box appears (see Figure 19.4).

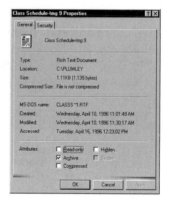

Figure 19.4 Set file attributes for individual files.

3. In the Attributes area, select Read-Only to prevent others from changing the file. Select Hidden to keep others from seeing the file.

4. Choose OK to close the dialog box and put the changes into effect.

Stopping Folder Sharing

You can also stop sharing an entire folder, which means it is no longer available on the network. To stop sharing a folder, you must be logged on as a member of the Administrators or Power Users group.

 Data Loss If you choose to stop sharing a folder while other users are connected to it, they may lose their data. NT warns you if any users are connected to the shared folder.

To stop sharing a folder, follow these steps:

1. Select the shared folder.

2. Choose File, Properties and select the Sharing tab.

3. Choose the Not Shared option and choose OK.

In this lesson, you learned to share folders and printers, change sharing properties, and stop sharing your resources. In the next lesson, you'll learn more about granting access and permissions, as well as how to secure files and folders.

SECURING FILES AND FOLDERS

In this lesson, you learn to grant permission for file and folder use, edit permission rights, and remove permissions.

UNDERSTANDING PERMISSIONS

You can establish permissions for every file or folder you create and for other shared resources (such as a network printer). Permissions set on files, folders, or other resources limit how much access individual users or groups of users have to that item. You can limit access so that another user can only view a file or folder, or you can allow unlimited access so that the user can add and delete files and folders, for example. You can even completely deny a person or group access to an object. Most permissions are set for entire groups instead of individual users, because that makes it easier for the system administrator to control overall access.

 Individual vs. Group   A user is an individual who generally works at one computer on the network (see Lesson 21). A group is defined within a Windows network as several users who work in a common manner or on similar projects. Often, permissions are granted to the group, which means that each user within the group has the same access to files, folders, and other resources.

Remember these important points when working with permissions:

- You can set permissions only on drives formatted with Windows NT File System (NTFS). Drives formatted with FAT (File Allocation Table) don't support Windows security; however, you can set permissions for shared folders on these drives.

- You cannot access or use a folder, file, printer, or ClipBook unless you have permission or belong to a group that has permission.

- Files and subfolders take on the same permissions as their parent folder.

- The creator of a file or folder is the owner; he or she can control access by changing permissions.

- Administrator group members can take ownership of a file or folder and then grant permissions to that file or folder.

NTFS or FAT?   NTFS is the Windows NT (New Technology) File System used with the Windows NT operating system. FAT (File Allocation Table) is the file system used with MS-DOS, and can also be used with Windows NT.

GRANTING PERMISSION FOR FILE USE

When you set permissions on a file, you're indicating the type of access a group or user has to that file. A file inherits its permissions from the folder if it's created in a folder.

UNDERSTANDING STANDARD FILE PERMISSIONS

You set file permissions from a standard list of permissions. Windows NT uses a set of abbreviations to indicate which permissions are granted. Table 20.1 lists the standard permissions for file access, their abbreviations, and a brief description of each permission.

TABLE 20.1 STANDARD FILE PERMISSIONS

PERMISSION	ABBREVIATION	DESCRIPTION
No Access	(none)	Prevents the user(s) from accessing the file
Read	RX	Permits the user(s) to view the file's data and run the file if it's a program file
Change	RWXD	Permits the user(s) to view the file's data, run it if it's a program file, change data in the file, and delete the file
Full Control	ALL	Permits the user(s) to view the file's data, run it if it's a program file, change data in the file, delete the file, change permissions on the file, and take ownership of the file

 TIP **No Access**   No Access permission overrides all other permissions.

SETTING FILE PERMISSIONS

As I mentioned earlier, you can set file permissions only on a drive formatted with the Windows NT file system. In addition, you must be the owner of the file to set permissions on it, or you must have been given Full Control access permission by the owner. To set permissions, follow these steps:

1. Select the file(s) in the Explorer right pane.

2. Choose File, Properties and then choose the Security tab. Choose the Permissions button and the File Permissions dialog box appears (see Figure 20.1).

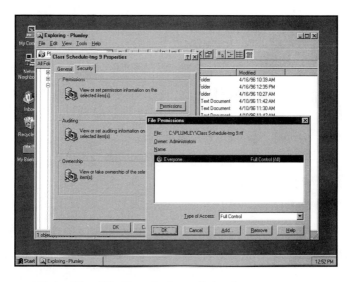

FIGURE 20.1 The File Permissions dialog box.

3. In the Name list box, select the user or group for whom you're setting permissions.

4. Choose the permission from the Type of Access box. If you want to remove file permissions instead, click the Remove button. If you choose to remove all permissions, no one but members of the Administrators group will have access to the file or folder.

5. Click OK to close the dialog box.

TIP   **Special Access**   To view the permissions set for any user or group, double-click the name in the Name list box. The Special Access dialog box appears, in which you can view and set other permissions.

GRANTING PERMISSION FOR FOLDERS

When you set permission on a folder, you limit the access that groups or users within the network have to that folder and its contents.

UNDERSTANDING FOLDER PERMISSIONS

You can set standard permissions for folders, and Windows NT uses abbreviations to indicate which permissions are used. Table 20.2 lists the standard permissions for folder access, their abbreviations, and a brief description of each.

TABLE 20.2   STANDARD FOLDER PERMISSIONS

PERMISSION	ABBREVIATION	DESCRIPTION
No Access	(none)	Prevents the user(s) from having any access to the folder and its contents
List	RX	Permits the user(s) to view folders, change subfolders, and view subfolders; does not permit access to the folder's files
Read	RX	Permits the user(s) to view file names and subfolder names, change subfolders, view data in the folder's files, and run programs

PERMISSION	ABBREVIATION	DESCRIPTION
Add	WX	Permits the user(s) to add files and subfolders to the folder; does not permit access to the folder's files
Add and Read	RWX	Permits the user(s) to view file names and subfolder names, change subfolders, view data in the folder's files, run program files, add files and subfolders to the folder
Change	RWXD	Permits the user(s) to view file names and subfolders, change subfolders, view data in the folder's files, run program files, add files and subfolders to the folder, change the folder's files, and delete the folder and its files
Full Control	ALL	Permits the user(s) to view file names and subfolders, change subfolders, view data in the folder's files, run program files, add files and subfolders to the folder, change the folder's files, delete the folder and its files, change permissions, and take ownership of the folder and its files

CHANGING FOLDER PERMISSIONS

You can change folder permissions only if you're the owner of the folder or if you've been granted permission by the owner. To set or change folder permissions, follow these steps:

1. Select the folder or folders in the Explorer window.

2. Choose File, Properties. The folder's Properties dialog box appears.

3. Choose the Security tab and the Permissions button. The Directory Permissions dialog box appears (see Figure 20.2).

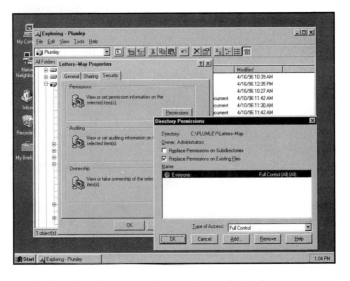

FIGURE 20.2   The Directory Permissions dialog box.

4. Choose one or both of the following check box options:

   Replace Permissions on Subdirectories   applies the permissions you select to all subfolders.

   Replace Permissions on Existing Files   applies the permissions you set to the folder and the files it contains.

5. Select the user or group in the Name list box and choose the permission from the Type of Access drop-down list box.

6. Choose OK to close the dialog box.

In this lesson, you learned how to grant permissions for file and folder use and how to edit and remove those permissions. In the next lesson, you'll learn to send and receive e-mail messages.

21 SENDING AND RECEIVING MAIL

*In this lesson, you learn to how to use the address
book, send and receive e-mail messages, delete a message,
and set options for the mail program in Microsoft Exchange.*

UNDERSTANDING MICROSOFT EXCHANGE

You use the Microsoft Exchange program to send and receive mail
messages within your network and over the Internet. This can be
done through memos, letters, and reports. You can even attach
files to a message. All messages sent in Microsoft Exchange travel
to a specified directory on your computer—usually
USERS\DEFAULT\WPGO, although it may be in another folder,
such as \EXCHANGE. Windows NT also refers to the process of
sending and receiving mail as Windows Messaging.

When you first start Microsoft Exchange, the Microsoft Exchange
Setup Wizard appears to guide you through setting up the program and creating a profile for yourself. Follow the directions and
make selections according to the suggestions in the Wizard dialog
boxes. If you have any questions, ask your mail or network administrator.

Internet Service Provider If you're setting up for the
Internet, you'll need to know your server's name or IP
address and your e-mail address, user account name,
and password. You can obtain this information from your
Internet service provider (IPS).

You can send and receive messages, delete and print messages, and set options in the Microsoft Exchange program. The following steps walk you through starting and exiting the program.

1. From the Desktop, choose the Start button, Programs, and Microsoft Exchange (your Microsoft Exchange may be in a folder, depending on your installation); alternatively, double-click the Inbox icon on your desktop.

2. If you've opened the program before, the Microsoft Exchange window appears (see Figure 21.1). The program opens to the same folder that was open the last time you used Exchange (the folder's name appears in the title bar).

3. To exit the program, choose File, Exit.

Folders list

Figure 21.1   Use the Microsoft Exchange program to send and receive e-mail.

Using the Address Book

The Address Book contains the names of the people in your workgroup on the network, as well as people in other domains and other workgroups. Although your system administrator creates and updates the Postoffice Address list, you can add or remove names on the list. You can also use the Address Book to add names to your personal address book.

To open and use the Address Book, follow these steps:

1. In the Microsoft Exchange program, choose Tools, Address Book. The Address Book appears with a list of names in the Postoffice List (see Figure 21.2).

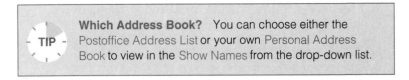

Which Address Book?   You can choose either the Postoffice Address List or your own Personal Address Book to view in the Show Names from the drop-down list.

FIGURE 21.2   The names of those in your workgroup appear in the Address Book.

2. To view more information about a user on the list (such as his or her phone number, office, or department), double-click the name.

3. To add a name to your personal address book, select the name and click the Add to Personal Address Book button.

4. When you're finished with the Address Book, click the Close button.

SENDING AND READING MESSAGES

You can compose a message, address it, send a carbon copy of it, and specify other options in the Send Note window of the Mail program. In addition, you can read the messages you've sent or received.

To create and send a message, follow these steps:

1. Choose Compose, New Message.

2. In the To text box, enter the name of the person to whom you're sending the message. Alternatively, you can click the To or Cc button and select the recipient's name from the list that appears. Separate multiple names with a semicolon.

3. In the Subject text box, enter the topic of your message.

4. In the message area, type your message. You are not limited to the space you see. As you type, the message scrolls upward in the box so you can fit more text in the message area.

5. Choose File, Send to send the message.

You can format the text in your message by selecting it and choosing the Format menu, and then Font or Paragraph; alternatively, use the formatting toolbar. Display the toolbar by choosing View, Formatting Toolbar.

New mail is displayed in your Inbox in bold type. To read a message you've received, follow these steps:

1. In the Microsoft Exchange program window, click the Inbox to display a list of received messages.

2. Double-click any message to read it.

3. To reply to the message, choose Compose, Reply to Sender. Type your reply and choose File, Send.

Send and Receive   To send and receive new mail, click the Tools menu and choose Deliver Now. If you're using more than one mail service, choose the Deliver Now Using command from the Tools menu, then choose the name of the service you're using from the secondary menu that appears.

Deleting a Message

In order to keep your messages from piling up, you should delete a message when you no longer need it. You can delete a message you've read by choosing File, Delete. In addition, you can delete any message from the message list by dragging it to the Deleted items folder.

If you change your mind and want the deleted message back, open the Deleted items folder by double-clicking it. Then select the message you want and drag it to another folder. If any messages remain in the Deleted Items folder when you exit the program, those messages are deleted permanently.

Setting Options

Microsoft Exchange provides several options you can set to customize the program to suit your tastes.

To change program options, follow these steps:

1. In the Microsoft Exchange program, choose Tools, Options. The Options dialog box appears (see Figure 21.3).

2. In the General tab, you can set the following options:

   When new mail arrives, play a sound, briefly change the pointer, or display a notification message.

   When deleting items, set the program to warn you before you permanently delete them and/or to empty the deleted items as you exit the program.

When starting the program, choose a profile for starting the program or choose to enter the profile when you first start the program.

FIGURE 21.3   Change Mail options to suit yourself.

3. In the Read tab, specify options for how the program deals with open items and forwarded items.

4. In the Send tab, specify options for sending mail, such as the font used, receipt requests, importance levels of the message, and so on.

5. Use the Services tab to add, remove, copy, and view properties of your mail services, including post office path, address book configuration, Internet servers, and IP addresses.

6. In the Delivery tab, specify a location for new mail and the order in which your information services are accessed.

7. Use the Addressing tab to control the post office and personal address lists.

8. Choose OK to close the dialog box.

In this lesson, you learned to send and receive mail messages over the network, as well as to delete messages, set mail options, and use the address book. In the next lesson, you learn to use the Internet Explorer program to access the Internet.

USING INTERNET EXPLORER

In this lesson, you learn how to use the Internet Explorer to browse the Internet.

ACCESSING THE INTERNET

You may have to try several times to attach to the Internet; in between tries you may need to edit your settings to get everything just right. When you're ready to access the Internet, follow these steps:

1. Open the Dial-Up Networking dialog box by double-clicking the icon in the My Computer window.

2. Click the Dial button and you'll see a **Connecting to** dialog box displayed; you can click the Cancel button at any time to stop the process.

3. If you chose to display a terminal window for logging on, enter the user name and password for your account and then choose the Done button. After you're verified on the server, the Connection Complete dialog box appears (see Figure 22.1). Choose OK to close the dialog box.

4. Double-click the Internet Explorer icon on your desktop to display a screen similar to the one in Figure 22.2; this is Microsoft's Start Page.

FIGURE 22.1   You're connected to the Internet.

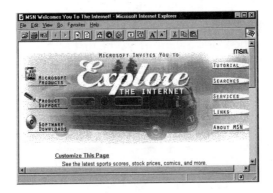

FIGURE 22.2   Time to Explore the Internet.

USING INTERNET EXPLORER

The Internet Explorer is a program that lets you access the Internet. You can access sites about books, people, countries, computers, and much more. This lesson assumes your Internet Explorer is set up and ready to go. If you need help setting up the Explorer, see Appendix B.

The Internet Explorer opens to the MSN (Microsoft Network) page. You can move the mouse around on the page and when the mouse pointer changes to a hand, that's a link to related information; most often, links are also underlined. You can click a link to see more information about that subject. For example, click the word Tutorial on the MSN screen to get an introduction to the

Web and ideas on searching for topics. Services gives you information about 800 numbers, area and country codes, zip codes, IRS tax forms, and more.

SEARCHING THE NET

You can quickly find Web pages about any topic by searching for the topic. Internet Explorer provides several different search types you can use and experiment with.

To search for a specific topic on the Internet, follow these steps:

1. Choose Go, Search the Internet; alternatively, you can choose the Searches button on the first MSN screen. Figure 22.3 shows the Search screen and explains some of the tool buttons you can use as you surf the Web.

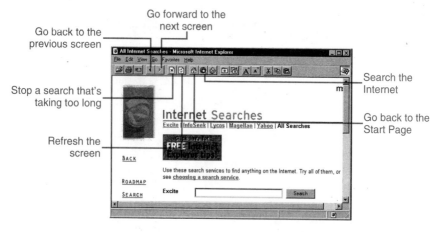

FIGURE 22.3 Surf the Web.

2. In the Excite text box, enter the topic for which you're searching and then click the Search button.

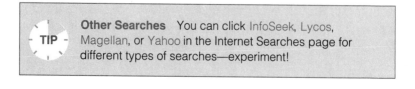

Other Searches You can click InfoSeek, Lycos, Magellan, or Yahoo in the Internet Searches page for different types of searches—experiment!

3. Results of the search display on-screen; you can continue to search or browse the information on the screen. Click the Back button to return to the Internet Searches page or choose link after link to just explore the Net.

SAVING PLACES FOR FUTURE ACCESS

You'll likely find Web sites that you will want to visit again. You can save the addresses to these sites so you can quickly go to them in the future.

To save a Web site to your Favorites folder, follow these steps:

1. While at the actual site, choose the Favorites menu and select Add To Favorites. Internet Explorer displays the Add To Favorites dialog box (see Figure 22.4).

FIGURE 22.4 Save your favorite sites for future reference.

2. In the Name text box, enter an easily recognizable name for the site or accept the default name.

3. Choose the Add button.

To access any of your favorite places, choose Favorites and select Open Favorites. The Favorites window appears from which you can select any site you've saved by double-clicking the site.

GOING TO A SPECIFIC SITE

If you know the address of the Web site you want to visit, you can easily go directly to that site. Follow these steps:

1. If the Address bar is not showing, choose View, Address Bar.

2. Enter the address in the Address text box and press Enter. The addresses you visit during one session are listed in the drop-down address list so you can go back to any of the listings at any time during your session.

WHEN YOU'RE DONE

When you're done surfing the Web and you're ready to disconnect from the net, you must exit Internet Explorer and hang up from the Dial-Up Networking dialog box. Follow these steps:

1. To exit Internet Explorer, choose File, Exit.

2. If the Dial-Up Networking dialog box is closed, open it again from the My Computer window by double-clicking the Dial-Up Networking icon. The Dial-Up Networking dialog box appears.

3. Click the Hang Up button. A message appears confirming you want to disconnect from your ISP's server; choose Yes. A beep signals you've been disconnected.

4. Close the Dial-Up Networking dialog box.

In this lesson, you learned to set up and use Internet Explorer. In the next lesson, you learn to use the Event Viewer to troubleshoot problems with Windows NT.

USING THE EVENT VIEWER

In this lesson, you learn to use the Event Viewer to troubleshoot problems you might have with Windows NT, the network, or your system.

UNDERSTANDING THE EVENT VIEWER

Use the Event Viewer is a program that monitors your system and records failures and problems in event logs. If, for example, a driver failed to load during startup or an application had a file error, the Event Viewer would record this event so you could study the problem.

Table 23.1 lists the common terms you'll see in the Event Viewer window.

TABLE 23.1 EVENT VIEWER TERMS

TERM	DESCRIPTION
Category	A classification that describes the event (such as Logon, Policy Change, or Account Management)
Computer	The computer name where the event occurred
Event	An identification number assigned to each event
Source	The software or system component that logged the event
User	The name of the user logged on at the time of the event

To start and quit the Event Viewer, follow these steps:

1. From the Desktop, choose the Start button, then choose
   Programs, Administrative Tools, and Event Viewer. The
   Event Viewer System Log appears (see Figure 23.1).

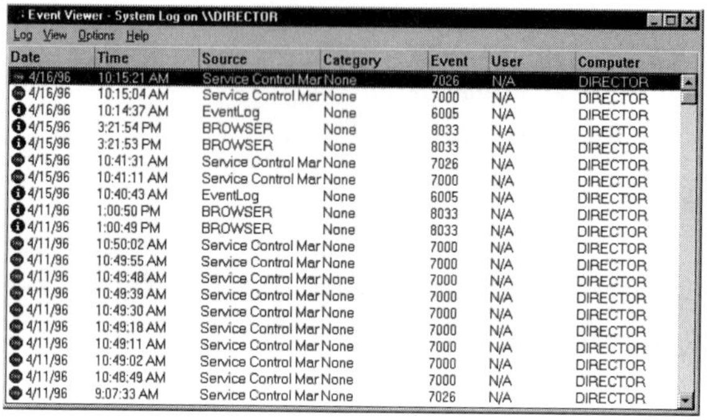

FIGURE 23.1 The Event Viewer starts recording events from the
first time you turn on your Windows NT Workstation.

2. To exit the Event Viewer, choose Log, Exit.

VIEWING EVENT LOGS

You can view three different logs in the Event Viewer: System,
Security, and Application. The System Log records events such as
hardware, driver, and other system component problems. The
Security Log records events such as breaches to security (attempts
to log on to the system, for example). The Application Log records
all application events, such as file errors, lockups, and so on.

To view an event log, follow these steps:

1. Open the Log menu.

2. Choose System, Security, or Application. A check mark
   appears beside the selected log, and the log name in the
   Event Viewer title bar changes.

3. You can choose View, Oldest First or View, Newest First to look at the logs in a different order by date. By default, the view shows the most recent events first.

4. To update the events shown in any Event Viewer log, choose View, Refresh.

The Event Viewer displays an icon to the left of each event to classify it. Table 23.2 describes the icons that appear in the Event Viewer log.

TABLE 23.2   EVENT VIEWER ICONS

ICON DESCRIPTION	EVENT TYPE	REPRESENTS
Stop sign	Error	A problem that leads to loss of data or functions
Exclamation point	Warning	Something that may cause future problems
Lowercase i	Information	An event that describes successful operation of major services
Padlock	Success Audit	Successfully audited security access attempt
Key	Failure Audit	Unsuccessfully audited security access attempt

Audit   The audit is a tracking service that follows the activities of users at the workstation and records selected events in the security log.

VIEWING EVENTS

You can filter the events in a log so that the Event Viewer displays only specific characteristics. In addition, you can search for specific events, and you can view descriptions and details of the events in any log.

FILTERING THE EVENTS

Filtering events is a way of displaying only the specific events you want to view. To filter events, follow these steps:

1. In the Event Viewer, pull down the Log menu and select the log you want to view.

2. Choose View, Filter Events. The Filter dialog box shown in Figure 23.2 appears.

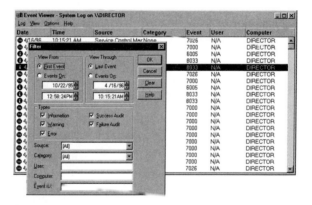

FIGURE 23.2   Choose specific characteristics to narrow the number and type of events displayed.

3. In the View From area, choose First Event to view events beginning with the first event ever logged on your system. Or, choose Events On to display only the events on and after the date and/or time you indicate in the text boxes.

4. In the View Through area, choose Last Event to view events through the most recent event on the system. Or, choose Events On to display events that were logged from the date and time you specified in the View From area to the date and time you specify in the View Through area.

5. In Types, deselect any type of event you do not want to view. By default, all event types are selected.

6. In the Source drop-down list, select the type of software (usually a device driver) you want to use to view the event.

7. In the Category drop-down list, choose one category to view only.

 TIP   **View User/Computer?**   In the User and Computer text boxes, you can choose to view events logged to a specific user or on a specific computer if you're not viewing your own and if you're logged in as a member of the Administrators group.

8. Click OK to apply the filtering options to the log. Figure 23.3 shows a system log with the information events filtered out.

Date	Time	Source	Category	Event	User	Computer
3/4/96	11:23:33 AM	Print	None	20	SYSTEM	DIRECTOR
3/4/96	11:19:58 AM	Service Control Mar	None	7026	N/A	DIRECTOR
3/4/96	10:41:52 AM	Service Control Mar	None	7026	N/A	DIRECTOR
3/4/96	10:41:50 AM	Server	None	2504	N/A	DIRECTOR
3/4/96	10:41:35 AM	Service Control Mar	None	7000	N/A	DIRECTOR
3/4/96	10:37:33 AM	Service Control Mar	None	7026	N/A	DIRECTOR
3/4/96	10:37:30 AM	Server	None	2504	N/A	DIRECTOR
3/4/96	10:37:14 AM	Service Control Mar	None	7000	N/A	DIRECTOR
3/4/96	10:30:35 AM	Service Control Mar	None	7026	N/A	DIRECTOR
3/4/96	10:30:32 AM	Server	None	2504	N/A	DIRECTOR
3/4/96	10:30:19 AM	Service Control Mar	None	7000	N/A	DIRECTOR
3/4/96	10:25:01 AM	Service Control Mar	None	7023	N/A	DIRECTOR
3/4/96	10:25:01 AM	Service Control Mar	None	7026	N/A	DIRECTOR
3/4/96	10:25:01 AM	Server	None	2503	N/A	DIRECTOR
3/4/96	10:25:00 AM	Service Control Mar	None	7001	N/A	DIRECTOR
3/4/96	10:24:59 AM	Service Control Mar	None	7001	N/A	DIRECTOR
3/4/96	10:24:59 AM	Service Control Mar	None	7002	N/A	DIRECTOR
3/4/96	10:24:52 AM	Service Control Mar	None	7001	N/A	DIRECTOR
3/4/96	10:24:52 AM	Service Control Mar	None	7000	N/A	DIRECTOR
3/4/96	10:24:52 AM	Nwlnkipx	None	9503	N/A	DIRECTOR

FIGURE 23.3   Filter out some events to make it easier to view problems.

FINDING EVENTS

Another way to view specific events is to use the Find feature, which is especially useful if your log is extremely large. You can, for example, search for all error events in all sources. To search for a specific event in a log, follow these steps:

1. In the Event Viewer, select the log you want to view.

2. Choose View, Find. The Find dialog box appears (see Figure 23.4).

FIGURE 23.4   Use the Find dialog box to find specific event types.

3. In the Types area, click the necessary check boxes so that only the events you're looking for have a check mark in the check box.

4. (Optional) To search through only a specific source or category, select the one you want from the Source or the Category drop-down list.

5. Choose Find Next when you're ready to search. The dialog box closes and highlights the next instance of the event type you're searching for.

6. Press F3 to find the next instance of the event type you described in the Find dialog box. Continue pressing F3 to search for the next instance.

VIEWING DETAILS OF AN EVENT

When you find some events (particularly a warning or an error, for example), you'll want to view more details of the event to get a clearer picture of what's going on with your system. You can view a text description of a selected event. However, be aware that some events generate more detail than others.

To view the details of an event, follow these steps:

1. In the Event Viewer, select the event you want to view.

2. Choose View, Detail. The Event Detail dialog box appears (see Figure 23.5).

 TIP   **Shortcut**   Double-click an event to quickly open the Event Detail dialog box.

FIGURE 23.5   You can view a description and other information about the event.

0000?   The information in the Data area of the Event Detail dialog box is binary data generated by the source of the event record. Usually, only a support technician familiar with the source can interpret this data. However, you can read the text description of the event and perhaps get a clue to your system's problem.

Changing Event Log Settings

You can change the settings of any Event Log. You can set the maximum log size, you can overwrite events as needed, and you can change other options as described in the following list:

- **Maximum Log Size**   Specify the maximum log file size, in kilobytes.

- **Overwrite Events as Needed**   Select this option to ensure that there will be space for new events when the log is full.

- **Overwrite Events Older than X Days Old**   Select this option to keep a log for a specific number of days (from 1 to 365).

- **Do Not Overwrite Events**   Select this to retain all events when log is full.

- **Default**   Click Default to restore default settings in the dialog box.

To change event log settings, follow these steps:

1. In the Event Viewer, choose Log, Log Settings. The Event Log Settings dialog box appears.

2. In Change Settings, select the log you want to change.

3. Change the settings as described in the previous list.

4. Click OK to close the dialog box.

In this lesson, you learned to use the Event Viewer to troubleshoot problems you might have with Windows NT, the network, or your system. In the next lesson, you learn how to configure and use NT's multimedia features.

WORKING WITH MULTIMEDIA

In this lesson, you learn to use CD Player, Media Player, and the Sound Recorder to work with multimedia.

USING THE CD PLAYER

Windows NT provides a CD Player program that works with your CD-ROM drive so that you can play audio CDs while you're working. Like a regular advanced CD player, Windows' CD Player contains features such as random play, programmable playback order, and the capability to save play lists. If you save a play list, you don't have to re-create it each time you insert a CD, which means you can skip over songs you don't want to play or you can play the songs in a specific order. To use the CD Player, follow these steps:

1. From the Desktop, choose the Start button, Programs, Accessories, Multimedia, and then the CD Player. The CD Player window appears (see Figure 24.1).

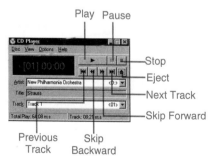

FIGURE 24.1 Use the CD Player to play music CDs on your computer.

2. Insert the CD into the drive, and the CD Player scans the
   CD. If you have played this CD before, the program fills
   in the artist, title, and track in the appropriate text boxes.
   If Autoplay is turned on, the CD will begin to play
   automatically after you insert it.

3. Click the Play button to play the CD, if Autoplay did not
   start it for you. To pause the CD, click the Pause button.
   To resume playing the CD, click the Play button again.

Skip Tracks   Choose the Track drop-down list to display
TIP   a list of tracks on the CD. Select a track and the CD
Player skips to that track.

4. If this is the first time you've played this CD, you can set
   up the play list by choosing Disc, Edit Play List. The CD
   Player: Disc Settings dialog box appears. Enter the artist's
   name and the CD title. In Play List, you can specify the
   order in which you want to play the tracks. Choose OK
   when you finish entering the settings.

5. To control the volume (you must have a sound card),
   choose View, Volume Control. The Volume Control box
   appears. Slide the bar up to increase the volume or down
   to decrease it.

Volume Control   The Volume Control box in the Acces-
TIP   sories window works the same as the Volume Control in
the CD Player. When the CD Player is on, you cannot use
the Volume Control box in the Multimedia folder.

6. To change the play order of the tracks, open the Options
   menu and choose Random Order. The CD Player mixes
   up the order of the tracks for you.

TIP   **Change Tracks**   Click the Previous Track button to play the previous track on the play list. Click the Next Track button to play the next track on the play list. Click the Skip Backwards button to move backward within a track. Click the Skip Forwards button to move forward within a track.

7. Click the Stop button to stop playing your CD.

8. Click the Eject button to eject your CD.

USING THE MEDIA PLAYER

The Media Player program enables you to play such multimedia files as Windows-compatible multimedia voice, animated video files, and MIDI-based music files. You might use the Media Player, for example, to view books, cartoons, or encyclopedia clips on CD. Figure 24.2 shows the Media Player. Depending on your computer, your Media Player may or may not look and work like the one described here.

MIDI File   A MIDI (Musical Instrument Digital Interface) file contains electronic instructions for playing music using different instrumental voices.

To use the Media Player, follow these steps:

1. From the Desktop, choose the Start button. Select Programs, Accessories, Multimedia, and then select the Media Player. The Media Player opens.

2. Open the Device menu and indicate which of the following you're going to play:

> **CD Audio**   Choose an audio CD to play.

> **Video for Windows**   Choose a video sequence (AVI); NT supports 8-bit, 16-bit, and 24-bit color image files.

If you choose a Video device, the Open dialog box appears. (If you choose CD Audio, you can insert an audio CD, and the Media Player begins playing the music.)

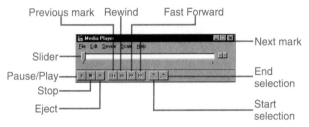

FIGURE 24.2 Use the Media Player to play sounds, video sequences, and even CDs.

3. In the Open dialog box, choose the drive, folder, and file name of the file you want to use. Then click OK.

4. In the Media Player, click the Play button to play the file.

5. To change the volume, choose Device, Volume Control. The Volume box appears. Adjust the volume by sliding the bar up for more volume or down for less volume.

Rewind and Fast Forward Drag the slider to the left to rewind to the previous selection mark or to the beginning of the file. Drag the slider to the right to fast forward to the next selection mark or to the end of the file.

6. Click the Stop button to stop playing your file.

7. Click the Eject button to eject your file (if it's on CD).

To play a specific selection, move the slider to the location where you want to start playing the selection. Click the Start Selection button to mark the beginning of the selection. Likewise, you can move the slider to the location where you want to stop playing the selection and click the End Selection button to mark the end of the selection. Press Alt+P or click the Play button to perform the selection you specified.

USING THE SOUND RECORDER

The Sound Recorder program lets you record, modify, and mix sounds. Figure 24.3 shows the Sound Recorder.

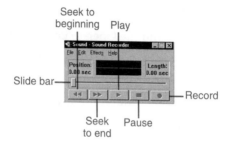

FIGURE 24.3   Use the Sound Recorder to create and modify sound files.

To be able to record sounds, you must have some type of input device such as a microphone or a MIDI instrument. You must also have a sound card, even if you're just recording a CD to a file.

To record a sound, follow these steps:

1. From the Desktop, choose the Start button. Select Programs, Accessories, MultiMedia, and then select the Sound Recorder. The Sound Recorder opens.

2. Choose File, New from the Sound Recorder menu bar. The Sound Selection dialog box appears.

3. Choose the Save As button and enter a name in the text box. Specify the file format and attributes. Choose OK.

4. In the Sound Recorder, click the Record button to begin recording.

5. Speak, play music, or make whatever sound you want to record into the microphone.

6. When you finish recording, click the Stop button to stop recording.

7. Choose File, Save As from the Sound Recorder menu bar to save the sound file. Enter a name and location for the sound file and choose OK.

To play a sound using the Sound Recorder, follow these steps:

1. From the Desktop, choose Start, Programs, Accessories, MultiMedia, and Sound Recorder.

2. Choose File, Open, and the Open dialog box appears.

3. Choose the drive, folder, and file name of the sound file you want to play. Then click the Open button.

4. Click the Play button in the Sound Recorder window to play the sound. As the sound plays, you see a visual representation of the sound waves in the Wave box, and the slide bar moves from the left to the right.

In this lesson, you learned to use the CD Player, Media Player, and the Sound Recorder. In the next lesson, you'll learn to use the Command Prompt.

USING THE
COMMAND
PROMPT

In this lesson, you learn how to use the command prompt, get help in a command prompt window, use DOS commands, and exit the command prompt.

UNDERSTANDING THE COMMAND PROMPT

The command prompt, or MS-DOS prompt, is a character-based interface to Windows NT. What that means is that you can type in commands at a prompt to perform tasks, to run applications, and to otherwise control the computer, your files and directories, and your programs.

You can use the command prompt to perform the following operations:

- Start applications usually associated with other operating systems (such as Windows NT, Windows 3.1, MS-DOS, or POSIX-compliant operating systems)

- Issue commands, including most MS-DOS commands and some new NT commands, as well as many network commands for using resources and administration

- Use the edit commands on the Control menu for cutting and pasting data between applications

> **Command Prompt** The Command prompt in Windows NT does not truly use MS-DOS; it actually uses a similar interface called the Windows NT command prompt. (The terms MS-DOS prompt and Command prompt, for all practical purposes, are the same.) If you type **ver** (for version) at the command prompt, NT responds with the prompt (**Windows NT Workstation 4.0**.) The prompt does, however, look and act like the command prompt you see in other operating systems.

To start and quit the command prompt, follow these steps:

1. From the Desktop, choose the Start button. Select Programs and from the Programs menu, choose Command Prompt. The Command Prompt window appears. As you can see in Figure 25.1, the default command prompt is the current drive and directory.

Figure 25.1   The Command Prompt window.

2. When you're ready to quit the command prompt, exit all applications (using each application's quit or exit command). Then type exit at the prompt and press Enter. You return to the Windows NT Desktop.

USING COMMANDS

There are hundreds of commands you can use at the command prompt and if you have questions about any of the commands, you can use the help feature as described in the next section. If you already know the DOS operating system, you can use many of the DOS commands you're used to. In addition, many NetWare commands work in the NT command prompt window.

Before I go into telling you about specific commands, though, let me tell you about a few things that relate to all commands. *Syntax* is the order in which you must type the command and any additional elements (command name, parameters, switches, and/or values) that follow it. A *parameter* is information that defines the object upon which you're performing a command, and a *switch* modifies how the command is performed. In the command **dir *.doc /s**, for example, **dir** is the command, ***.doc** is the parameter, and **/s** is the switch. This command tells Windows NT to list a directory of all documents with a .DOC extension found in all subdirectories.

Table 25.1 describes a few of the more common commands you may find a use for.

TABLE 25.1   COMMON COMMANDS

COMMAND	PARAMETER(S)	FUNCTION
break		Stops the previous command
cd\		Changes to the root directory
cd	*subdirectory*	Changes to the specified subdirectory
cls		Clears the screen
copy	*file drive\directory*	Copies the specified file to the specified drive and/or directory

continues

TABLE 25.1 **CONTINUED**

COMMAND	PARAMETER(S)	FUNCTION
dir		Displays a list of files and subdirectories in the current directory
erase	*file(s)*	Deletes one or more specified file(s)
move	*file drive\directory*	Moves the specified file to the specified drive and/or directory
ren	*oldfilename newfilename*	Renames the file specified by oldfilename with the name specified by newfilename
start		Starts a separate window in which to run a command or program
edit		Starts the MS-DOS Editor, in which you can create and edit text files
exit		Closes the command prompt window

To use a command, first start a new MS-DOS session by clicking the MS-DOS icon in the Program Manager's Main program group window (as covered in the previous section). Type the command and any additional parameters or switches at the command prompt, and then press Enter. Figure 25.2 shows the Command Prompt window with the results of the command dir *., which displays a list of directories only.

Directory list —

FIGURE 25.2   The DIR command offers many parameters and switches that enable you to display the directories on your computer.

TIP

Slow Down!   When you list a directory, it usually scrolls by so quickly that you can't read everything on the list. To fix that, type dir /p. The /p stands for "pause," which tells Windows NT to pause the listing a screen at a time so you can see everything in the list. When the list is paused, you can press any key to continue to the next screen.

Error Message   If, after entering a command, you receive a message that says the name specified is not recognized, you may have misspelled the command or used the wrong parameters. Try entering the command again. If you continue to have problems, check the online Help system, which you'll learn about next.

GETTING HELP

Just as you can get online Help by using the commands in Windows NT's Help menu, you can get online help for all commands at the command prompt. Table 25.2 describes the common Help commands you can type at the command prompt.

TABLE 25.2   HELP COMMANDS

COMMAND	FORM OF HELP PROVIDED
help	Displays names of the 32-bit operating system commands
command /?	Gives you help on the syntax, parameters, and switches for the command you enter (for example, if you type **dir /?**, it gives you help on the **dir** command)
net help	Lists the names of the network commands
net help command	Lists the syntax, parameters, and switches for network commands

RUNNING APPLICATIONS IN THE COMMAND PROMPT WINDOW

You can install applications from the Command Prompt window, and you can run MS-DOS and Windows applications in the Command Prompt window. To run a program from the command prompt, follow these steps:

1. From the Desktop, open the Start menu; choose Programs, and then choose the Command Prompt. The Command Prompt window appears.

2. If necessary, use the cd command to change to the directory holding the program you want to start. For example, to change to the WordPerfect directory, you'd type **cd\wp60** and press **Enter**.

3. At the prompt, enter the program name that starts the program (for example, you'd type **wp** to start WordPerfect).

TIP   **MS-DOS Window?**   You can manipulate an MS-DOS window similarly to other windows; you can minimize, maximize, restore, and move a Command Prompt window. In addition, check out the Control menu for other features.

COPYING AND PASTING FROM THE COMMAND PROMPT WINDOW

You can select text or graphics in any application open in the Command Prompt window, and you can copy or cut it and paste it into another application or document. Using the copy and paste procedures, you can copy data from one MS-DOS program and paste it into another MS-DOS program or a Windows application.

To copy and paste data, follow these steps:

1. In the Command Prompt window, open the application and the document from which you want to copy data.

2. Select the data to copy using the Edit, Mark command and click the Command Prompt window's Control-menu button.

3. Select Edit, Copy. Windows NT copies the data to the Windows Clipboard.

4. Switch to the window of the application and document to which you want to paste the copied data. You can use the Task bar to switch to either a Windows application or an application in another Command Prompt window.

5. Position the insertion point in the location where you want to add the data, and then choose Edit, Paste. (If the application is in a Command Prompt window, click the Control-menu button and choose Edit, Paste instead.)

In this lesson, you learned to start and quit the command prompt, enter commands at the command prompt, access online help from the command prompt, and start an application from the command prompt. In the next lesson, you'll learn to customize the look of Windows NT.

CONTROLLING THE APPEARANCE OF WINDOWS NT

26

In this lesson, you learn to change desktop colors, add wallpaper and patterns to your desktop, and use a screen saver.

OPENING THE CONTROL PANEL

You use the *Control Panel* to control such aspects of Windows NT as the colors, fonts, modems, sounds, and so on. Figure 26.1 shows the Control Panel window; some of your icons may differ from those in the figure.

FIGURE 26.1 Control your hardware, sounds, colors, and so on using the Control Panel icons.

To open the Control Panel, follow these steps:

1. Choose the Start button.

2. Select the Settings menu, Control Panel. To open any icon in the Control Panel, double-click that icon.

CHANGING THE COLOR SCHEME

You can change the color scheme that Windows NT uses for your desktop, windows, menus, title bars, and so on, to a preset color scheme. To change the Windows NT color scheme, follow these steps:

1. In the Control Panel, open the Display icon by double-clicking it.

2. Choose the Appearance tab. Figure 26.2 shows the Display Properties dialog box with the Appearance tab displayed.

FIGURE 26.2 Use the tabs in the Display Properties dialog box to control the features pertaining to the desktop.

3. From the Scheme drop-down list, select a color scheme. The sample at the top of the dialog box shows what the new colors in the windows and desktop will look like.

4. Check out as many different color schemes as you want. When you're satisfied with the selected color scheme, click OK. If you plan to make other changes to the Display Properties dialog box (in other tabs), choose the Apply button to accept the changes made to the Appearance tab and continue.

Default Colors If you want to go back to the scheme
TIP originally on your computer, choose Windows Standard if
you've already made a change. If you have not made a
change and you don't want to, choose Cancel.

ADDING WALLPAPER AND PATTERNS

You can choose from a variety of designs to apply to your desktop
using the Desktop icon in the Control Panel. Figure 26.3 shows
the Background tab of the Display Properties dialog box and its
options.

FIGURE 26.3 Use the Background tab to add wallpaper or
patterns to your desktop.

ADDING WALLPAPER

Wallpaper consists of colorful, *bitmapped images* that you display
on your desktop for decoration.

Bitmapped Images   Bitmap is a file type used for storing images. Because the image is stored as a series of dots, called *pixels*, the image has rough edges and shows few details.

To apply a wallpaper design to your desktop, follow these steps:

1. In the Display Properties dialog box, choose the Background tab.

2. In the Wallpaper section, scroll the list and select the wallpaper design you want to use.

3. Click the Center option button to have Windows center one small icon from the file in the center of the desktop screen. Click the Tile option button to have Windows repeat the wallpaper icon so that the entire desktop is filled with the pattern.

4. Choose OK to close the dialog box and accept the wallpaper design. Alternatively, click the Apply button to accept this change and continue making changes to the Display Properties dialog box.

Why So Slow?   If you notice that your computer reacts more slowly than it did before, that's because using wallpaper and/or patterns for your desktop requires extra memory. If you're low on memory, you may want to use only a solid color for your desktop.

Adding Patterns

Patterns are additional designs you can apply to your desktop for decoration. To apply a pattern, follow these steps:

1. In the Display Properties dialog box, choose the Background tab.

2. In the Pattern area of the dialog box, scroll the list and choose the pattern you want to use.

3. (Optional) Choose the Edit Pattern button and change the pattern by clicking the mouse in the pattern box. As you add to the design, the Sample box changes to reflect your additions. To remove an addition, click the box a second time. Choose Change to accept the changes and Done to close the Edit Pattern dialog box. If you do not want to save your changes, choose Done and when prompted to save, choose No.

4. Choose OK to close the Display Properties dialog box. The pattern appears on your desktop.

TIP **You Can't Use Both** If you select both a pattern and a wallpaper in the Desktop dialog box, the wallpaper overlays the pattern.

ADDING A SCREEN SAVER

Even though screen savers are no longer needed to prevent damage to your monitor from *burn-in*, they're still fun to use. If you select a screen saver, Windows runs a pattern across your screen anytime your computer is inactive for the specified length of time. To return to the screen and continue working, you simply press a key or move the mouse.

To select a screen saver, follow these steps:

1. In the Display Properties dialog box, choose the Screen Saver tab. Figure 26.4 shows the Screen Saver tab of the Display Properties dialog box.

2. In the Screen Saver section, open the drop-down list and choose a screen saver.

Burn In   In older monitors, extremely light screens (such as those you see in Windows) had what is called a burn-in effect. When a Windows screen was left on the computer for a long period of time, the Windows image burned into the monitor. Then when the monitor was turned off or used in DOS, a ghost of the Windows screen remained. Screen savers were originally used to keep the burn-in effect from ruining monitors. Newer monitors have built-in protection against burn-in.

FIGURE 26.4   Change screen savers periodically, just for fun.

3. Click the Preview button to view a sample of the screen saver to make sure you like it. When you finish viewing the screen saver, click the mouse button to return to the Desktop dialog box.

4. In the Delay text box, enter the number of minutes you want Windows NT to wait for your computer to be inactive before it starts the screen saver.

5. (Optional) Choose Password Protected if you want your screen saver to remain on-screen until you enter your password. This prevents other individuals from viewing your screen without your knowledge.

6. (Optional) Choose the Settings button to set any specific options that deal with your selected screen saver. Then choose OK to close the Settings dialog box.

7. Choose OK to close the dialog box and accept the changes. The next time you leave your computer inactive for the specified amount of time, the screen saver you selected appears on your screen.

In this lesson, you learned to change your desktop colors, add wallpaper and/or patterns to your desktop, and use a screen saver. In the next lesson, you'll learn to control some hardware settings (including setting the date and time and your modem).

LESSON 27

CONTROLLING HARDWARE SETTINGS

In this lesson, you learn to change the date and time and modify mouse and modem settings.

ALTERING THE DATE AND TIME

You use the Control Panel to set your computer's system date and time, which is used to time-stamp files as you create and modify them. In addition, many applications allow you to automatically insert the date and time on-screen or when you print, so you'll want to be sure to have the right time on your computer.

 Bad Battery? If you set your date and time and then find that the date is wrong when you start your computer again, you probably have a bad battery.

To check or set the date and time, follow these steps:

1. From the Desktop, open the Start menu, choose Settings and Control Panel.

2. In the Control Panel window, double-click the Date/Time icon. The Date/Time Properties dialog box appears with the Date & Timer tab selected (see Figure 27.1).

3. In the Date area, select the correct month and year from the drop-down lists; then click the day on the calendar.

4. To change the time, click the portion of the time you want to change and either enter the correct number or use the spinner arrows to increase or decrease the value accordingly.

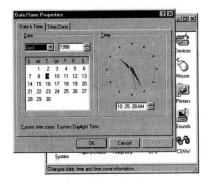

Figure 27.1 The Date/Time Properties dialog box.

5. (Optional) Choose the Time Zone tab and check the Automatically Adjust for Daylight Savings Changes check box (put a check mark in it) if you want Windows to change the time automatically in the fall and spring.

6. Select OK or press Enter to accept the changes you have made. Select Cancel or press Esc to close the dialog box without saving changes.

TIP **Time Zone** If necessary, use the Time Zone drop-down list to change your current time zone. You might use this option if you move or travel with your computer.

MODIFYING MOUSE SETTINGS

The mouse settings enable you to change tracking, to choose a double-click speed, and to swap the left and right mouse buttons. Figure 27.2 shows the Mouse Properties dialog box.

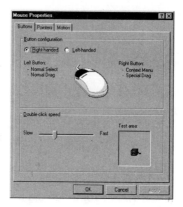

FIGURE 27.2   Adjust the mouse settings to better suit your needs.

By double-clicking the Mouse icon in the Control Panel, you access the Mouse Properties dialog box, where you can modify the following settings for your mouse:

Pointer Speed   (Motion tab) Use pointer speed when you're working on a notebook or laptop computer. The speed adjusts the rate at which the pointer travels across the screen, making it easier to find your pointer on the small screen. Set the speed to Slow if you have trouble seeing the mouse pointer; set the speed to Fast if the "slow-motion" mouse is distracting.

Pointer Trail   (Motion tab) If you use a notebook or laptop computer, you can choose to display a trail, or echo the pointer, to help you find the pointer on a small, poor-resolution screen. Choose Short for a brief trail or Long for an extended trail.

Double Click Speed   (Buttons tab) Adjust the speed to suit your finger's double-click speed. Slower means you can actually perform the two clicks more slowly. Adjust the speed and then test in the TEST box.

Swap Left/Right Buttons   (Buttons tab) Check this box to switch buttons, if you're left-handed or just more comfortable with the switch.

Use the Pointers Tab   The Pointers tab of the Mouse
Properties dialog box enables you to change your mouse
pointers to look like dinosaurs, hands, and other icons.
To view the different icon types, select an item from the
Scheme drop-down list. Icons in the sample box change
to reflect the selected scheme.

To modify the mouse settings, follow these steps:

1. From the Desktop, open the Start menu and choose
   Settings, Control Panel.

2. In the Control Panel window, double-click the Mouse
   icon to open the Mouse Properties dialog box.

3. Adjust the settings.

4. Select OK or press Enter to accept the changes you have
   made. Select Cancel or press Esc to close the dialog box
   without saving changes.

CONFIGURING YOUR MODEM

If you have a modem attached to your computer, you can modify
the settings. Additionally, you can add or remove modems easily
using the Modem Wizard.

ADDING A MODEM

Before adding a modem, connect the modem to your machine, if
it's external, and turn it on. If you've added an internal modem,
make sure it's properly connected.

To add a modem, follow these steps:

1. From the Desktop, open the Start menu and choose
   Settings, Control Panel.

2. Double-click the Modem icon to open the Modems
   Properties dialog box (see Figure 27.3)

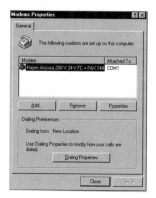

Figure 27.3   Configure your modem in the Modems Properties dialog box.

3. To add a new modem, choose the Add button. The Install New Modem dialog box appears, as shown in Figure 27.4.

Figure 27.4   Adding a modem is as easy as following directions.

4. Let NT detect your modem by choosing the Next button; then follow the directions on-screen to complete the installation.

When NT returns to the Modems Properties dialog box, you can configure the dialing properties, as described in the next section, or you can choose the Close button to return to the Desktop.

TIP   **Too Many Modems?**   To remove a modem you no longer use, open the Modems Properties dialog box and select the modem from the list. Choose the Remove button. Choose Close to return to the Desktop.

MODIFYING DIALING PROPERTIES

Dialing properties control how your calls are dialed. You may never need to modify these properties; however, if you're using a notebook and you use your modem from the road, hotels, and so on, you'll want to change dialing properties when you change locations.

To modify dialing properties:

1. In the Modems Properties dialog box, choose the Dialing Properties tab.

2. In the Dialing Properties dialog box, choose the My Locations tab, as shown in Figure 27.5.

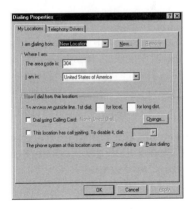

FIGURE 27.5   Use dialing properties when you go on the road with your notebook computer.

3. In the **Where I Am** area of the dialog box, enter the ZIP code and country from which you are calling.

4. In the **How I Dial From This Location**, enter the
following information, as required:

> **To Access An Outside Line** If you must first
> dial a number to access an outside line (as is often
> required in hotels), enter that number in this area;
> note you can enter a number to dial to access a local
> and/or long distance line.
>
> **Dial Using Calling Card** Choose the Change but-
> ton to enter your calling card number, if you want to
> use a card when dialing from this location.
>
> **This Location Has Call Waiting** If the location
> from which you're calling has call waiting, enter the
> code to disable that feature while you're calling with
> a modem.
>
> **The Phone System At This Location Uses**
> Choose either Tone or Pulse dialing.

TIP   **Come Here Often?** If this is a location you often make
modem calls from, you can save these settings for the next
time you need to make a call. At the top of the dialog box,
choose the New button. The text in the I Am Dialing From
text box becomes selected; enter the location name to
save it, such as Bill's Office or Dartmouth Hotel-PA. Press
Enter to accept the changes and close the dialog box.

5. Choose OK to accept the changes and close the dialog
box; choose Close to close the Modems Properties dialog
box.

CHANGING MODEM PROPERTIES

You also can modify certain modem settings as port, speed, and
connection from the Modems Properties dialog box. Figure 27.6
shows a Hayes modem Properties dialog box; although each modem will have similar settings, the Properties boxes representing
each brand or type of modem may look slightly different.

FIGURE 27.6   Make changes to your modem's configuration.

To change modem properties, follow these steps:

1. In the Modems Properties dialog box, select the modem you are configuring from the list so the modem's name is highlighted.

2. Choose the Properties button. Make any changes as follows:

> Port   Choose the port to which your modem is connected, usually a COM (communications) port.

> Speaker Volume   A personal preference; in most cases, you can turn the speaker volume off and adjust the volume. The sounds that come through the speaker are communication sounds between your modem and another; you can tell when the modems connect by listening to the sounds.

> Maximum Speed   Set the highest speed at which your modem can communicate. Your modem will adjust speed if the modem to which you're connecting runs at a slower speed.

> Connection Preferences   (on the Connections tab). These include data bits, parity, and stop bits settings. See the documentation of your ISP, BBS, or other network you're trying to connect to for this information.

Call Preferences   Choose whether to wait for a dial tone before dialing, the amount of time to wait before disconnecting if nothing is sent back and forth between the modems, and the amount of time to wait before canceling the call if connection doesn't take place.

TIP   Questions?   If you have any questions about your modem's configuration, read the documentation that came with it.

3. Choose OK when finished setting the modem's properties. Choose Close to exit the Modems Properties dialog box.

In this lesson, you learned to change the date and time, modify mouse settings, and configure your modem.

INSTALLATION TROUBLE-SHOOTING

During the installation of Windows NT Workstation, you might run into some potential roadblocks. For example, you might be asked for some hardware information that you do not readily know, or you might run into some problems with the installation itself. This appendix offers some help for installing Windows NT Workstation.

WHAT YOU NEED TO KNOW

To save time during installation and to avoid frustration, gather the facts you need before you begin the installation. The inside front cover of this book gives you the basic steps for installing Windows NT Workstation, but there is much more to it than just those few steps. If you have any doubts, ask your system administrator. You will need all of the following information in order to install Windows NT Workstation:

- The type of network adapter card you have, as well as the card's interrupt request number (IRQ) and base I/O (Input/Output) address will be very important. Consult the documentation that came with your network card for this information.

- Your computer name and workgroup or domain name will be needed.

- The printer model and the port to which it's connected (if you have a printer connected directly to your computer).

- Whether you want to create a dual boot and preserve the existing operating system within a partition, or to reformat the drive to a Windows NT Workstation operating system is important. You can designate a portion (partition) of the drive as MS-DOS and a portion as Windows NT. Your decision depends on the type of programs you use, your network logons, and other factors. If you're unsure, see your system administrator.

- Which network protocols to install to be compatible to the network to which you're attached.

Floppy Disk   You will need a high density floppy disk on which to create an emergency repair disk during Windows NT installation. You can use the disk later to get into Windows NT if you have a problem with the program.

Installing Windows NT Workstation from a CD

After you complete the installation steps in the inside front cover of this book, you begin installing Windows NT Workstation using either a CD or Setup Disk 4. The first problem may occur if NT Setup prompts for Setup Disk 4 instead of reading your CD. If this happens, it means that your CD-ROM device is not a supported device. Windows NT supports only SCSI CD-ROM devices. If your CD-ROM is not a SCSI, you must install Windows NT Workstation in a different way.

If your CD-ROM device is supported in MS-DOS, you can install Windows NT Workstation from MS-DOS. If you do, your drive will use dual boot and the FAT file system instead of the NTFS. FAT (File Allocation Table file system) and NTFS (NT File System) are two different methods operating systems use to organize the files on disk. The NTFS system offers more security options when used with Windows NT. Your network and your system administrator will probably have a preference for the type of file system you use, so you should ask him or her before you install Windows NT. Alternatively, you can install Windows NT Workstation from the network. Ask your system administrator for more information.

To install Windows NT using an unsupported CD-ROM device, follow these steps:

1. Exit Setup by following the directions on-screen. Prepare three formatted high-density disks you can use during setup, plus an extra disk for an emergency repair disk. Label the disks Setup Boot Disk, Setup Disk #2, Setup Disk #3, and Emergency Repair Disk.

2. In MS-DOS, insert the Windows NT Workstation CD into the CD drive. At the MS-DOS prompt, type the CD drive letter and the directory name **I386**. For example, if your CD drive letter is **D**, type **D:\I386** and press Enter.

3. At the prompt, type **winnt** and press Enter. The CD begins setup. During setup, you will be prompted to insert each floppy disk in turn. Windows NT Workstation Setup copies files to the floppy disks and to your hard disk.

4. When it finishes copying files, Setup asks you to press Enter to restart the computer. Press Enter.

5. The computer reboots, and Setup asks you to insert the Setup Boot Disk. When you do, Setup begins installation of the Windows NT Workstation files. Follow directions on-screen to complete the installation.

 No CD-ROM Drive?!   Windows NT will not recognize your CD-ROM drive after installation if the drive is not supported. You might be able to acquire an updated driver that will work with Windows NT from the drive's manufacturer.

TROUBLESHOOTING INSTALLATION

You could run into a host of hardware or software problems during installation. These are just a few of the possibilities, along with some suggestions that might make for a smoother installation. As always, if you need more help, see your system administrator.

IRQ Conflicts

Interrupt conflicts are problems that occur when two hardware devices are trying to share the same IRQ settings. It is important to keep notes on the IRQ settings each component of your computer uses to ensure that you don't assign the same address to two devices. Generally, Windows NT Workstation Setup will suggest settings and identify conflicts. However, if a device does not seem to be working, you'll want to check your settings to make sure there are no conflicts. You can find out a hardware's settings by referring to that hardware's documentation.

Problems with Fax/Modems or Other Devices

Some peripherals (such as a non-SCSI CD-ROM device) may not be supported by Windows NT Workstation and, therefore, may not work. You can contact the manufacturer of the device to see if they have an updated driver that works with Windows NT.

Displays, Drivers, and Monitors

At one point during the installation of Windows NT Workstation, Setup asks you about your monitor's resolution. Be very careful when changing options in that Setup dialog box. Windows NT suggests a configuration and asks you to test it. If you do not have a good reason to change the configuration, and the test looks okay to you, do not change anything in the dialog box.

If you change drivers and you choose the wrong one for your video card, your computer may not restart correctly. If that happens, choose the VGA boot option on the Boot Loader starting screen, and then manually set the video driver in the Control Panel. You may need to ask for assistance from your system administrator.

SETTING UP THE INTERNET EXPLORER

APPENDIX

B

Setting up Windows NT to use the Internet Explorer
is not an easy task. You must install the protocol as well as Dial-Up
Networking and you'll need to find out the settings for your Internet
service provider's server, IP address, and so on. This lesson introduces
you to the steps you need to complete to prepare to use the Internet
Explorer; however, you may need more help before you're ready to
connect.

> **TIP**
>
> **Help!** For more help on getting ready to connect to the
> Internet, check out the online help in NT. Searching for
> Internet in the Help Index, then click connecting to.

Before you connect to the Internet, you need to complete the
tasks outlined in the following general steps:

1. Connect and then install a modem to your computer (or
   access to a modem over your network). Set up a modem
   in the Control Panel by double-clicking the Modem icon
   and following directions to the Add Modem wizard.

2. Get an Internet account with an Internet service provider
   (ISP). You'll need to know the following: user name, password, access phone number, the host's name and domain
   name, the Domain Name Server (DNS) server address, IP
   address, authentication procedure, Subnet Mask, and
   Default Gateway. Choose a PPP (Point-to-Point) account,
   if your provider offers it.

3. Install the TCP/IP protocolTCP/IP protocol to your workstation from the Control Panel, Network icon. In the Pro-

tocols tab, choose the Add button and select the TCP/IP
Protocol. When prompted to use the DHCP to configure
the TCP/IP protocol automatically, choose Yes.

4. In the Network dialog box, Protocols tab, choose the TCP/
   IP Protocol and select the Properties button. In the IP
   Address tab, choose to Specify an IP Address and fill in
   the information as given to you by your ISP (see Figure
   B.1). Choose OK when you are done. You'll be prompted
   to restart your computer, but wait; there are other settings
   to configure first.

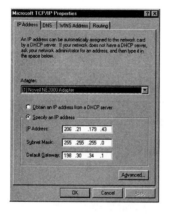

Figure B.1   Fill in the information for your Internet server.

 IP Addresses? Subnet Mask?   The configuration settings you enter into the Dial-Up Networking and TCP/IP
Properties dialog boxes are each unique. The numbers,
separated by periods, identify the network to which the
server is attached and the server itself.

5. Install the Dial-Up Networking, if it is not already installed. In the Control Panel, use the Add/Remove Programs icon to install Dial-Up Networking. You'll need the

Windows NT Workstation CD to complete installation. When next you're prompted to restart the computer, do so.

6. In My Computer, double-click the Dial-Up Networking icon and follow the directions for setting up your connection to the access provider. You'll need to know the ISP's phone number, server type, whether you'll need a terminal window to log on, and so on. Figure B.2 shows the completed Dial-Up Networking dialog box.

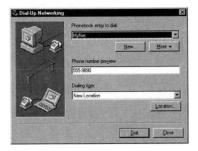

Figure B.2   You're ready to dial your Internet service.

 Trouble?   If you have trouble connecting to your Internet service and you need to edit settings, choose the More button in the Dial-Up Networking dialog box and select Edit Entry and Modem Properties.

INDEX